Academy Governance Checklists

Gillian Allcroft

icsa

The Governance
Institute

First published 2019

Published by
ICSA Publishing Limited
Saffron House, 6–10 Kirby Street
London EC1N 8TS

Typeset by Patricia Briggs
Edited by Sheida Heidari
Cover designed by Anthony Kearney

British Cataloguing in Publication Data
A catalogue record for this book is available from the British Library.

ISBN 978-1-86072-767-2

Table of Contents

About the author

Gillian Allcroft has worked in education policy for 30 years and spent the last 15 focusing on governance. She is the former deputy chief executive of the National Governance Association and a recognised expert in school and academy governance.

Gillian started her career in the Department for Education and then in 2004 left to join the National Governors' Council which subsequently became the National Governance Association. She is the author of *Welcome to a Multi-Academy trust: A guide for newly appointed trustees* – an induction guide for trustees. Gillian has been a regular speaker at events relating to school and academy governance.

Foreword

The range of governance tasks and activities to be undertaken within the academy trust setting is wide-ranging and varied. On any given day, those responsible for delivering governance in an academy trust might be working on board support, policies, admissions, data protection, freedom of information, risk or annual reports.

Trusts report to multiple regulators and are committed to ensuring transparency of governance arrangements. This is crucial to ensuring information is readily available to the school's community, parents and the wider public. In practical terms however, this means that even a relatively simple task such as appointment of a new trustee requires multiple steps including securing internal approvals, submission of filings with two regulators and updating information on the trust's website and register of interests.

As anyone who has worked in academy governance, or dedicated time as a volunteer trustee or local governor will know, navigating the range of guidance that sets out academy governance requirements can take time. The requirements are also nuanced according to whether the trust is a single or multi-academy trust.

Whether you are appointing an accounting officer or wondering about your website compliance requirements, the useful checklists held within this publication will therefore provide a vital shortcut for the reader. They will ensure that academy governance professionals do not need to reinvent the wheel by creating their own checklists for key processes, so that their time can be invested in strategic and impactful governance initiatives that will make a real difference to their trusts and the young people they support.

Anna Machin
Governance Manager, Ark Schools

Preface

The *Academy Governance Checklists* provides a handy, quick reference guide to the most common academy governance and administrative processes. The book is intended not as a definitive legal guide, but as a handy reference document which will assist users in establishing and following proper procedures in line with good practice. It has been cross-referenced to the DfE and ESFA's statutory guidance and advice, Charity Commission and Companies House guidance, ICSA's *Academy Governance Handbook* and relevant legislation, all of which provide more detailed information on a number of the topics covered.

Each topic comprises a short explanation of the particular issue, a checklist of items to be considered, any procedural steps to be taken, filing requirements (DfE/ESFA and/or Companies House) as well as some general notes and cross-references.

The checklists should not be regarded as exhaustive and given the freedom of academy trusts to set their own operating processes do not have to be followed slavishly but are intended to act as a guide for the user, highlighting procedures that should be considered in the context of that topic.

The book has been prepared for all academy trusts, which are all charitable companies limited by guarantee. While academy trusts are exempt charities, they are still subject to charity law and as private companies subject to relevant company law as well as education legislation and DfE/ESFA requirements. Some sections will be relevant to MATs rather than SATs.

This text will be of particular interest to clerks and governance managers of SATs and MATs. It covers the key governance issues likely to face an academy trust and provides answers to procedural questions likely to be raised. Clerks/governance managers will find it particularly useful when advising their trustees on specific issues.

It may also be of interest to accounting officers who have an important role in advising the board and in many cases act as trustees, providing a quick reference on key issues enabling AOs to ensure papers for the governing board cover the salient points and enable better discussion.

Finally, trustees may find it useful to dip into the book when faced with a particular issue; it can point you in the right direction for further advice and guidance.

Academy trusts are charitable enterprises, funded almost exclusively by the public purse and responsible for educating the nation's children. They are rightly subject to high levels of scrutiny and it is important that they not only follow proper procedures, but that they do so in accordance with good governance principles.

I hope that this publication can assist those responsible for governance in academy trusts in their endeavours.

Gillian Allcroft

Acronyms and abbreviations

AC	Academy committees
AFH 2018	Academies Financial Handbook
AGM	Annual General Meeting
AO	Accounting Officer
AP	Alternative provision academies
ARD	Accounting reference date
ASP	Analyse School Performance
CA2006	Companies Act 2006
CEO	Chief Executive Officer (in a MAT)
CFO	Chief Financial Officer
CIF	Condition Improvement Fund
CPD	Continuing professional development
DBS	Disclosure and Barring Service
DfE	Department for Education
DPO	Data protection officer
EAL	English as an additional language
EEF	Education Endowment Foundation
EHCP	Education, Health and Care Plan
ERG	External review of governance
ESFA	Education & Skills Funding Agency
FNtl	Financial Notice to Improve
FOI	Freedom of Information
FSM	Free school meals
GAG	General annual grant
GDPR	General Data Protection Regulation
GIAS	Get information about schools
HSE	Health and Safety Executive
ICO	Information Commissioner's Office
ICSA	The Institute of Chartered Secretaries and Administrators
KCSIE	Keeping children safe in education

LA	Local Authority
LAAP	Local Authority Associated Persons
LGB	Local Governing Body (in a MAT)
MAT	Multi-academy trust
NFF	National funding formula
NGA	National Governance Association
NLG	National Leader of Governance
NSS	National Support School
OFSTED	Office for Standards in Education
PFI	Private Finance Initiative
PSC	Persons of significant control
PTA	Parent Teacher Association
RPA	Risk Protection Arrangement
RSC	Regional Schools Commissioner
SAIL	Single alternative inspection location
SARA	Sector annual report and accounts
SAT	Single academy trust
SCA	School condition allowance
SENCo	Special educational needs co-ordinator
SEND	Special educational needs and disabilities
SIC	Standard industrial classification
SORP	Statement of Recommended Practice
UTC	University Technical College
VAT	Value added tax

Academies Financial Handbook

Introduction

The Academies Financial Handbook (AFH 2018) is produced annually by the Education and Skills Funding Agency (ESFA). All academy trusts are required by their funding agreements (see page 145) to have regard to the guidance in the document.

The title is slightly misleading as although its major function is to set out financial requirements, it also covers governance and staffing.

Checklist

▶ All senior executive leaders and trustees should read the document annually.

▶ Check that the requirements within the AFH 2018 relating to governance/trustee responsibilities have been met.

▶ The AFH 2018 recommends that there is separation between those who are members of the trust and those who are also trustees/ directors – check whether there is any overlap.

▶ Ensure that all trustees and any non-trustees sitting on trustee board committees which relate to finance are aware of the requirements in the AFH 2018.

▶ The trustee board must establish an audit committee.

▶ If the trust's income is more than £50 million the audit committee must be separate to any finance committee.

▶ The trustee board should establish a finance committee.

▶ Check who sits on the finance and audit committees to see whether the composition meets the requirement of the AFH 2018.

▶ Check that the trustee board has met the requirements of the AFH 2018 in relation to the appointment of a senior executive leader.

▶ Check that the trustee board has a written scheme of delegation of financial powers.

▷ Check that the ESFA's Accounting Officer's annual letter to accounting officers has been shared with trustees.

Notes

▷ All funding agreements require academy trusts to conduct their business within the terms and requirements of the AFH. It is consequently the 'quickest' way for the DfE/ESFA to 'direct' academy trusts to act in a certain way. This is why the document has come to include more on governance as it is the only means of directing change, short of enacting legislation.

Academies general

Introduction

Academies are state-funded independent schools in England. The responsibility for the schools is vested in an academy trust; this can be a single academy trust (SAT) responsible for one school or multi-academy trust (MAT) responsible for more than one school. In both cases the trust is a charitable company limited by guarantee. Academy trusts are exempt charities and their principle regulator is the Department for Education (DfE).

Schools within a MAT have no separate legal entities; the trustee board is the responsible and accountable authority.

The legislation under which Academies were originally created was the Learning and Skills Act 2000, which the Academies Act 2010 then built on to open academy status to many more schools.

Checklist

The various forms of academies are:

- Academy – this is a mainstream primary or secondary phase school which converted from a maintained school.

- Alternative Provision Academy – this is an academy for children and young people who have been excluded from other schools, usually but not exclusively mainstream schools.

- Free School – this is an academy which is new to the state-funded sector. It could be in response to the need for additional school places in a local authority area, or in response to an application by a group seeking to extend choice in an area or it could be an independent fee-paying school transferring into the state sector. Studio Schools and University Technical Colleges (UTCs) are specific types of free schools.

- Special Academy – these are academies specifically for children and young people with special educational needs and disabilities. They will usually 'specialise' so that they cater for children with similar forms of SEND (e.g. autism).

▶ Studio School – these are small schools (usually with around 300 pupils) teaching mainstream qualifications through project-based learning. This means working in realistic situations as well as learning academic subjects. Students work with local employers and a personal coach, and follow a curriculum designed to give them the skills and qualifications they need in work, or to take up further education.

▶ UTCs specialise in subjects such as engineering and construction – and teach these subjects along with business skills and using IT. Pupils study academic subjects as well as practical subjects leading to technical qualifications. The curriculum is designed by the university and employers, who also provide work experience for students. They are sponsored (i.e. established) by universities, employers or further education colleges.

▶ Students are admitted at age 13/14 to both Studio schools and UTCs and this had made it challenging for them to thrive, as in most cases students start secondary school at age 11 and there is a reluctance to change school again at 14. Several of both have closed as a result of lack of numbers.

Procedure

▶ There are set procedures to be followed to apply for academy status or open a new school.

▶ For an academy to be established an academy order must be granted by the Secretary of State for Education. This can be done in a variety of ways:

▷ the governing body of a maintained school may apply to convert to academy status;
▷ a school which is deemed to be inadequate by Ofsted following an inspection will automatically be the subject of an academy order; and
▷ sponsors/an existing academy trust can apply to open a new school.

Notes

▶ Although legally still possible, in reality the DfE is highly reluctant to accept applications from single schools to convert to academy status. All schools wishing to convert are encouraged strongly to do so with a group of schools and form a MAT or seek to join an existing MAT.

More Information

▶ *Academy Governance Handbook*, Chapter 1.

Academy committee – decision-making powers/ terms of reference

Introduction

ACs exist at individual academy level in MATs. They are committees of the trustee board and have no powers in their own right.

A MAT's trustee board is the legally accountable body for all decisions taken in the trust. This does not mean that the trustee board needs to take all decisions; many can and should be delegated, to the chief executive, other staff, trustee committees and ACs. Some trusts delegate monitoring and scrutinising functions to the ACs, but no specific decision-making powers.

Checklist

▶ The trustee board must determine what functions will be delegated to ACs.

▶ Delegated decision-making powers must be recorded in the SoD.

Procedures

▶ The trustee board must decide annually on the composition and terms of reference for ACs. This must be done at a properly constituted and quorate trustee meeting. Decisions must be recorded in writing in the SoD.

▶ The trustee board must set down the procedures under which ACs will operate and which, if any, decisions they are entitled to make.

Notes

▶ What is delegated to AC level is very much a matter for the trustee board and will vary depending on the culture of the board, the geographical spread of the MAT, the number of schools and the number of pupils. In general, the larger the MAT the more likely it is to need to delegate some functions to ACs or cluster committees.

More information

▶ *Academy Governance Handbook*, Chapter 6.

Academy committee – general

Introduction

Academy committees (ACs) exist at school level in MATs. In articles of association they are usually, although not exclusively, referred to as local governing bodies (LGBs) but many MATs have also renamed them advisory or academy councils (AdCos) (AcdCs).

The articles of association for MATs will certainly provide for ACs to exist. Usually it is for the MAT trustee board to decide whether each academy school needs its own AC, whether there should be one AC over several schools, or whether there should be any ACs at all.

Checklist

▶ Check your articles of association to see what they say about the establishment of ACs.

▶ Ensure your scheme of delegation (SoD) for governance functions is clear about what decision-making powers, if any, are delegated to ACs.

▶ Ensure that there is no duplication between the functions being carried out by the trustee board and ACs.

Notes

▶ In larger MATs it is simply not possible for the trustee board to monitor and scrutinise academy level detail in the same way as the trustee board in a SAT or a small MAT can. But this monitoring of school level details still needs to be carried out. This is the function of ACs. There are a range of functions they can fulfil. These are:

  ▷ gaining an understanding of how the school is led and managed;
  ▷ monitoring the implementation of trust policies and whether the school is meeting agreed targets;
  ▷ establishing whether school finances are managed well;
  ▷ engaging with local stakeholders;
  ▷ being a point of consultation and representation; and
  ▷ reporting to the board.

▶ Not all ACs will have all these functions and it is important to note that whatever they are called these bodies are committees of the trustee board and have no powers beyond those granted to them by the trustee board (see also scheme of delegation). The trustee board has the power to remove these delegated functions at any time.

▶ In small MATs it is possible to govern without ACs.

▶ It is vital that the division of responsibilities between the trustee board, the executive and ACs is clear and set out explicitly in the SoD. Lack of clarity in the SoD has been a common problem across many MATs and leads to confusion, misunderstanding and sometimes mistrust.

▶ It is important to establish good levels of communication between the trustee board and any ACs, which allow for both upwards and downwards communication.

Academy committees (composition, appointment, removal, resignation and term of office)

Introduction

ACs exist at individual academy level in MATs. They are usually referred to as local governing bodies (LGBs) but many MATs have also renamed them AdCos or AcdCs. They are committees of the trustee board and have no powers in their own right.

Checklist

▷ Check what the articles of association say about the composition of ACs.

▷ The trustee board must establish written procedures covering the appointment, removal and terms of office of those sitting on ACs.

▷ These must be communicated clearly to those sitting on ACs.

▷ The SoD must set out who is responsible for the appointment and removal of those sitting on ACs.

Composition

▷ As there are several iterations of articles of association the precise rules in relation to the composition of ACs vary.

▷ In MATs created before 2010 the composition of the ACs is often entirely at the discretion of the trustees (and sometimes the Principal Sponsor), with no specific requirements.

▷ In most MATs established after 2010 the rules governing who sits on the trustee board have an effect on the composition of ACs. The Articles for these MATs specify that if there is no provision for elected parents on ACs, or if there are no ACs established, then there must be two elected parent trustees. Many MATs choose to have elected parents at AC level, even if they also have parent trustees.

▷ There is no requirement for ACs to include any trustees.

▷ Some articles of association specify a maximum size for ACs, but in most cases this is at the discretion of the trustee board.

▷ In trusts containing UTCs there will be specific provisions giving the 'employer sponsor' and the 'university sponsor' the power to appoint a majority of either the trustee board or the AC.

Appointment

▷ As these are 'special' committees of the board there are few, if any, rules laid down in articles of association about appointments.

▷ If the articles require that there are either parents on the trustee board or on the AC, then these positions must be elected. The elected or appointed parent trustees must be a parent, or an individual exercising parental responsibility, of a registered pupil at one or more of the academies at the time when he is elected or appointed. A parent can only be appointed if not enough parents stand for election.

▷ It is a matter for the trustee board to decide the maximum size of the AC and how other committee members should be appointed. After the initial establishment of an AC the trustee board can choose to retain responsibility for appointments or can delegate that responsibility to the AC.

▷ The trustee board should determine the procedure for appointment – i.e. application form, skills audit, interview – which either it, or the AC, will use to appoint people to the AC.

▷ These procedures should be in writing and the SoD should make clear who has the power to make decisions.

▷ In many cases the trustee board delegates responsibility for finding and recommending candidates to the AC with the trustee board having ultimate approval of the candidate.

Chair and vice chair – appointment

▷ The trustee board can choose to retain this power or delegate. The SoD must set out who is responsible, i.e. have the trustees retained the power or have they delegated it to the AC.

▷ How this works and how long chairs and vice chairs can serve in the position needs to be set out in the procedures.

Removal

▷ Those sitting on ACs are not trustees or directors and have no formal 'governance' position. It is for the trustee board to determine procedures for removal.

▷ The trustee board retains the power to change the procedures for appointment and removal of those at AC level and indeed whether ACs should exist at all.

Resignation

▷ Those serving on ACs can resign at any point.

Term of office

▶ It is for the trustee board to determine how long the term of office for those sitting on ACs will be. Generally, these are either three or four years.

Procedures

▶ These will be as established by the trustee board in accordance with any stipulations in the articles of association.

Notes

▶ It is currently unusual in school governance (whether academy or maintained) for the constitution documents to specify a maximum length of service for those sitting on the board or ACs. It is however considered good governance practice (see Charity Governance Code). As it is for the trustee board to set procedures for appointments and removals to ACs they can introduce such a rule.

Filing requirements

▶ Details of those sitting on ACs must be reported to the ESFA via the DfE's Get information about schools (GIAS) website.

More information

▶ Academy Governance Checklists:

▷ Academy committee – general;
▷ Academy committee – decision-making powers/terms of reference;
▷ Delegation of authority;
▷ Scheme of delegation (of government functions).

▶ *Academy Governance Handbook*, Chapter 4.

Academy trust

Introduction

An academy trust is the legal entity which runs an academy school or schools. Those responsible for single schools are known as SATs and those responsible for several multi-academy trusts MATs, or MACs (multi-academy companies) in the case of Catholic MATs.

All academy trusts are charitable companies limited by guarantee. They are exempt charities, meaning that the Secretary of State for Education is their principal regulator – this duty is carried out by the DfE and ESFA.

Academy trusts sign a formal contract with the DfE, known as the funding agreement (see page 145). This sets out that the DfE commits to funding the academy trust providing that in turn the trust meets the obligations placed on it by the funding agreement. MATs will have a master agreement and supplementary agreements for each academy.

The academy trust's governing document is its articles of association. The articles describe how the trust will be governed, including how many members and trustees can be appointed and by whom, their voting rights and so on.

All academy trusts have two formal layers of governance: members (see page 188) and directors/trustees (see pages 113 and 286). MATs may also have ACs at academy level.

Members are not exclusive to academy trusts – most charitable companies have members as a result of the requirements of the Companies Act 2006 (CA2006). The first members are the signatories to the memorandum of association drawn up when the trust formed. These members will also have agreed the trust's first articles of association, which include the trust's charitable objects – i.e. the purpose of the organisation. While members hold the trustee board to account for the effective governance of the trust, the members themselves have a minimal role in the actual running of the trust.

All academy trusts are governed by a board; as charitable companies the people sitting on this board have dual functions as charity trustees and company directors. They are subject to both charity law and company law. The board is responsible for the general control and management of the administration of the charity and must always act in the best interests of the charity.

The DfE generally uses the term 'trustees' to refer to the people on the board. In MACs these people will always be referred to as directors.

Checklist

▶ All academy trusts must meet the filing requirements of the CA2006 in relation to limited companies.

▶ Members and trustees need to understand the importance of their articles of association.

Accounting officer

Introduction

Accounting officer (AO) is a formal designation. The AO role in a public sector organisation carries significant responsibility and the AO is the person who parliament calls to account for the stewardship of its resources. The role is usually held by the most senior officer in the organisation; in the case of academy trusts, this is the senior executive leader (see page 267).

The academy trust is required by its funding agreement to appoint an AO, who must be assigned the duties set out in the AFH 2018 and Chapter 3 of HM Treasury publication *Managing Public Money* and notify the Secretary of State of their name.

The role of AO includes specific responsibilities for financial matters. It includes a personal responsibility to Parliament, and to the ESFA's accounting officer, for the financial resources under the trust's control. AOs must be able to assure Parliament, and the public, of high standards of probity in the management of public funds, particularly regularity, propriety and value for money. AOs must also adhere to the 'seven principles of public life'.

Checklist

▶ The academy trust must appoint a named AO, who should be the senior executive leader.

▶ The accounting officer must have appropriate oversight of financial transactions.

▶ The accounting officer must ensure that the academy trust's property and assets are under the control of the trustees, and measures exist to prevent losses or misuse.

▶ The AO must ensure that bank accounts, financial systems and financial records are operated by more than one person.

▶ The AO must ensure that the trust keeps full and accurate accounting records to support their annual accounts.

▶ The AO must complete and sign a statement on regularity, propriety and compliance each year and submit this to the ESFA with the audited accounts.

▶ The AO must also demonstrate how the trust has secured value for money via the governance statement in the audited accounts.

▶ The AO must take personal responsibility (which must not be delegated) for assuring the board that there is compliance with the funding agreement and handbook.

▶ The AO must advise the board in writing if any action it is considering is incompatible with the articles, funding agreement or handbook.

▶ The AO must advise the board in writing if the board fails to act where required by the funding agreement or AFH 2018. Where the board is minded to proceed, despite the AO's advice, the AO must consider the board's reasons and if the AO still considers the action proposed by the board is in breach of the articles, the funding agreement or AFH 2018, the AO must notify the ESFA's AO immediately in writing.

Procedure

▶ The trustee board must confirm the appointment of the AO at a properly constituted and quorate meeting.

Filing requirements

▶ The ESFA must be notified via the GIAS website.

More information

▶ AFH 2018.

▶ HM Treasury, *Managing Public Money*: www.gov.uk/government/publications/managing-public-money

▶ *Academy Governance Handbook*, Chapter 12.

Accounting reference date

Introduction

All companies, whether trading or not, must prepare accounts and file a copy with the Registrar of Companies. The accounts are prepared in respect of each accounting period. Accounting periods begin at the conclusion of the previous period, or the date of incorporation and the end of the accounting reference date. Companies House will automatically set the accounting reference date to the first anniversary of incorporation.

Academy trusts are also subject to their funding agreement and the AFH 2018. Academy trusts with open academies do not set and cannot change their accounting reference period. The accounting reference date is set by the DfE as the academy financial year which runs from 1 September to 31 August.

Academy trusts which exist as companies but do not have any open academies still need to comply with company law – their accounting reference date may be different to 31 August.

Accounts must be produced and audited for the accounting period ending on 31 August as a condition of the funding agreement unless the DfE has specified, exceptionally and in writing, that another date can be adopted. Academy trusts that become inactive must prepare accounts for the period where a funding agreement and open academies are in place, and after this date continue to follow company law requirements.

Checklist

▷ New academy trusts with open academies must ensure that the accounting reference date is changed at Companies House to 31 August.

▷ Arrange for annual report and accounts to be prepared to meet accounting reference date.

Filing requirements

▷ New trusts must change the accounting reference date at Companies House.

More information

▷   *Academy Governance Handbook*, Chapter 12.

Accounts – Academies Accounts Direction

Introduction

The Academies Accounts Direction is the reference pack produced by ESFA for academy trusts and their auditors to use when preparing and auditing financial statements for the accounting period ending on 31 August annually.

To produce the Accounts Direction the ESFA adapts the Charity Commission's (for England) SORP and adapts it to the circumstances of academy trusts.

The Accounts Direction sets out everything that academy trusts must include in their annual reports and financial statements and the accounting treatments required. It also provides a model format for the report and the financial statements to ensure consistency of treatment between academy trusts.

Checklist

▶ Academy trusts must comply with the instructions in the Academies Accounts Direction pack.

Notes

▶ The accounts direction pack is updated annually and academy trusts and their auditors need to ensure they are using the latest version.

More information

▶ DfE Academies Accounts Direction pages: www.gov.uk/guidance/academies-accounts-direction

Accounts – academies consolidated annual report and accounts

Introduction

Academies consolidated annual report and accounts (also known as the Sector Annual Report & Accounts (SARA)) are produced by the DfE and provide an overview of all academy schools in England. They fulfil the reporting requirements of section 11 of the Academies Act 2010, under which the Secretary of State for Education must prepare, publish and lay an annual report on academies in England before Parliament and the government financial reporting manual (FReM) to report on academy finances. They are produced in line with the accounts direction issued by HM Treasury.

Academy trusts must fill in an accounts return to the ESFA (as well as submitting their audited accounts). The accounts return is used by the DfE to complete the SARA. They must also fill in the land and buildings collection tool (see page 181).

The accounts return requires additional information to that included in academy trusts' annual reports and financial statements. The additional information is required because of the different reporting standards used by the DfE and academy trusts. As charitable companies academy trusts are required to prepare their annual reports and financial statements using the SORP, but the DfE in common with all government departments reports against the International Financial Reporting Standards. As academy trusts are directly funded by the government, the DfE must provide financial reports on the entirety of the academy estate.

Checklist

▷ The accounts return must be submitted to the ESFA in the January following the end of the financial year.

▷ The accounts return must be signed off and submitted by the academy trust's auditors.

Procedure

▶ Both the accounts return and land and buildings collection tool are online returns. The ESFA publishes updated guidance each year on how to complete and submit them.

Notes

▶ Up to the year 2015–16 the consolidated academy accounts were included as part as the DfE's own accounts but since then have been produced as a separate dedicated sector report. One of the main reasons for this was the disparity between the DfE's own financial year 1 April–31 March and academy trust financial year, which is 1 September–31 August. The complexity of attempting to reconcile these two sets of returns meant that it was difficult for both the National Audit Office (NAO) and Public Accounts Committee (PAC) to assess their accuracy and the DfE was criticised for not being able to assure Parliament about the proper use of public funds.

More information

▶ SARA – www.gov.uk/government/collections/academies-sector-annual-reports-and-accounts

Accounts – annual accounts return

Introduction

The accounts return is required by the ESFA in order for it to be able to produce the academies' SARA (see page 18).

The accounts return is an online form which must be submitted annually, currently in the January following the end of the financial year.

The accounts return requires additional information to that included in academy trusts' annual reports and financial statements. The additional information is required because of the different reporting standards used by the DfE and academy trusts. As charitable companies academy trusts are required to prepare their annual reports and financial statements using the SORP, but the DfE in common with all government departments reports in accordance with the International Financial Reporting Standards. As academy trusts are directly funded by the government, the DfE also must provide financial reports on the entirety of the academy estate.

The ESFA provides detailed guidance, updated annually, on what needs to be included.

Checklist

▷ All academy trusts must prepare and submit the accounts return (this includes new trusts which may not have been in operation for a full year and thus not have published audited accounts).

▷ The accounts return must be completed and sent to the academy trust's auditors to be submitted to the ESFA by the required deadline.

More information

▷ ESFA pages: www.gov.uk/guidance/academies-accounts-return

Accounts – annual requirement

Introduction

Academy trusts are publicly funded charitable companies running state-funded schools. As a result, there is considerable interest in the way in which they use their funds and quite rightly there is a requirement from the DfE and ESFA that academy trusts publish an annual report and audited accounts, as well as submitting additional information for publication in the SARA.

Checklist

▸ Academy trusts must prepare annual reports and accounts for each Academy Financial Year in line with the ESFA's accounts direction.

▸ The academy trust must prepare and file with Companies House the annual reports and accounts required by the CA2006 within nine months of the end of the financial year (usually May).

▸ Academy trusts' accounts must be audited annually by independent auditors appointed in line with the AFH 2018.

▸ The academy trust's annual report must include a governance statement.

▸ The academy trust's annual report must include the names of all members of the academy trust who served during the year.

▸ The accounts must carry an audit report stating whether, in the opinion of the auditors, the accounts show a true and fair view of the academy trust's affairs. The accounts must also be supported by such other audit reports, relating to the use of grants and other matters, as the Secretary of State directs.

▸ Academy trusts must produce a statement of regularity, propriety and compliance, and obtain a regularity assurance report on this statement from the auditor.

▸ Academy trusts must submit their annual report and audited accounts and auditor's regularity assurance report to the ESFA within four months of its year-end, usually by 31 December.

▷ Academies are required to publish their annual report and accounts on their website by 31 January.

Procedure

▷ Following appointment of auditors the chief financial officer (CFO) should arrange for the annual audit to meet AFH 2018 timescales.

Accounts – approval

Introduction

In accordance with the CA2006, academy trusts' annual report and accounts must be approved by the board of directors, which for academy trusts is the same as the board of trustees.

The annual report and accounts, once approved by trustees, must be sent to all members.

Checklist

▶ Be clear about who must approve the accounts.

▶ Trustees' report must be signed by a named trustee and dated.

▶ Statement of Regularity, Propriety and Compliance must be signed by the accounting officer.

ss. 414(1) and 419 (1) Companies Act 2006

▶ The governance statement must be signed by a trustee and accounting officer.

▶ The balance sheet must be signed by a trustee.

ss. 414(2) and 43 (1) & (2) Companies Act 2006

▶ The audit report must be signed by the independent auditors.

▶ Ensure that the annual return and audited accounts are sent to members.

ss. 503–505 Companies Act 2006

Procedure

▶ Convene a trustees' meeting to approve the annual report and accounts.

▶ Ensure the registered company number is included and is correct.

▶ Circulate copies of the annual report and accounts to the members.

▶ Arrange filing at Companies House.

▶ Arrange submission to the ESFA.

▶ Publish the annual report and accounts on the academy trust's website.

Filing requirements

▶ The annual report and accounts must be filed with Companies House within nine months of the end of the financial year – usually 31 May for academy trusts.

▶ The annual report and accounts must be filed with the ESFA (as principal regulator) within four months of the end of the financial year – usually 31 December.

Accounts – dormant

Introduction

Where a company has not traded during any particular financial period, the company can dispense with the obligation to prepare audited accounts and need only file an abbreviated balance sheet and a signed statement by a trustee/director to the effect that the company was dormant during the period.

If an academy trust has been inactive for the full period between its incorporation date and the end of the relevant academy financial year, it is termed 'dormant'; and it can apply s. 480 of the CA2006 and prepare dormant accounts. To be classed as dormant the academy trust must not have made any transactions in the period.

An academy trust that transferred its last academy to another academy trust before the previous year-end may also produce dormant accounts if it had no transactions for the year.

If an academy trust prepares dormant accounts it must report to a period end date of 31 August 2018. Academy trusts that are dormant for only a portion of the period up to 31 August 2018 will instead need to produce full audited accounts.

Submission and publication of dormant accounts is subject to the same deadlines as full accounts, including submission to the ESFA for assurance purposes within four months, usually by 31 December.

Notes

▶ Dormant academy trusts are most likely to be those given approval to set up, but for whatever reason not yet running any, academy schools.

More information

▶ ESFA academies accounts direction.

▶ Companies House – guidance on filing accounts.

Accounts – filing period

Introduction

There are time limits for filing annual accounts with Companies House and with the charity regulators (i.e. ESFA).

s. 453 Companies Act 2006

Accounts must be prepared in respect of each accounting period. Accounting periods begin at the conclusion of the previous period, or the date of incorporation and end of the accounting reference date (see page 15).

There are strict timescales for the filing of accounts and both Companies House and the ESFA can take action if accounts are submitted late. In the case of Companies House companies will be fined when accounts are filed late (see page 27). The ESFA may issue a Financial Notice to Improve (FNtL) (see page 137).

Accounts must be received by the filing date – i.e. proof of postage is not enough.

Checklist

▷ Academy trusts (as private companies) must file their accounts within nine months of the accounting reference period, unless it is the first accounting period and is for a period greater than 12 months – the deadline is three months after the period or end of 21 months from the date of incorporation, whichever is later.

▷ The filing deadline is calculated to the same date in the month as the accounting reference date. If that is the last date of the month then the filing period ends on the last day of the appropriate month – i.e. as the accounting reference date for academy trusts is 31 August, the filing deadline with Companies House is 31 May.

▷ Academy trusts must file their accounts with the ESFA within four months of the end of the financial year – i.e. for most trusts by 31 December.

AFH section 2.8 and ESFA academy accounts direction

Notes

▷ The ESFA suggests that academy trusts file their accounts with Companies House immediately after they publish on their website – i.e. by 31 January – although the legal requirement is to file them by 31 May.

Accounts – late filing penalty

Introduction

Companies House has a sliding scale of fines which will be applied if accounts are not submitted on time. Directors of the academy trust are responsible for ensuring returns are filed on time with Companies House.

s. 44(1) Companies Act 2006

Time after the deadline	Penalty (for private limited companies)
Up to 1 month	£150
1 to 3 months	£375
3 to 6 months	£750
More than 6 months	£1,500

Academy trusts with open academies who do not meet the requirement to submit their accounts to the ESFA by 31 December may be subject to a FNtI (see page 137). The ESFA may also publish a list of any defaulters.

Notes

▷ The penalties are imposed on the company not the individual directors and are a civil matter. Under certain circumstances directors can be prosecuted for failure to submit accounts on time. This is a criminal offence and if convicted carries a penalty of a maximum fine of £2,000 for each offence.

▷ Late filing penalties are doubled if a company files its accounts late in two successive financial years.

Accounts – related party transactions

Introduction

Related party transactions are financial transactions in which the academy trust has made payments to someone who is closely connected to the trust. This could be a payment to someone directly involved in the administration or management of the trust – i.e. a member, trustee, those sitting on academy committees, or someone closely related to them, or a firm with which they have a close connection or controlling interest.

Both charity and company law require that trustees act in the best interest of the organisation, not the individuals involved in its administration or management. Both require that conflicts of interest are managed and preferably avoided.

Academy trusts are publicly funded charitable companies and there is a keen interest and scrutiny in how they use their money. Any suggestion that those involved in running the trust are financially benefiting from that involvement is severely frowned on. Where there is a possibility that the interests of a trustee and the trust may conflict, the trustee must declare the conflict.

The SORP and Academies Accounts Direction require that related party transactions are publicly declared in the audited annual accounts.

Checklist

▷ The academy trust's register of interest must record the relevant business and pecuniary interests of members, trustees, AC members within a MAT and senior employees, including:

> ▷ directorships, partnerships and employments with businesses;
> ▷ trusteeships and governorships at other educational institutions and charities; and
> ▷ for each interest: the name of the business; the nature of the business; the nature of the interest; and the date the interest began.

▷ The annual accounts must include disclosure of any related party transactions, including:

▷ the names of the related parties and a description of the relationship between them;

▷ a description of the transactions and the amounts involved;

▷ the amounts due to or from the related parties at the balance sheet date, and any provision for doubtful debts or amounts written off;

▷ details of any guarantees given/received;

▷ terms and conditions, including whether they are secured, and the nature of the consideration to be provided in settlement; and

▷ other elements of the transactions which are necessary for the understanding of the accounts.

▶ Where the goods or services exceed £2,500 academy trusts must provide a note stating that anything above £2,500 is provided a cost, which must be accompanied by a statement of assurance from the related party confirming this.

▶ Academy trusts must also describe how the transaction has been managed, e.g. what procurement process was followed in order to demonstrate it meets financial regularity standards.

▶ Incoming (e.g. donations of goods, services or property) and external (e.g. purchase of goods, services or property) must be recorded separately.

▶ The note should include any transaction with connected charities that meets the definition of s. 28 of schedule 3 of the Charities Act 2011.

▶ If there are no related party transactions this must also be stated.

Notes

▶ The rules on related party transactions have been revised and tightened over several years. Academy trusts must keep up to date with the rules on approving and recording related party transactions. From April 2019 the rules changed with related party transactions over £20,000 requiring approval from the ESFA.

▶ The ESFA explains how 'at cost' should be calculated in the AFH 2018.

More information

▶ Academies Accounts Direction.

▶ AFH 2018.

Admissions – pupil admission arrangements

Introduction

All state-funded schools in England have published admission arrangements. Admission arrangements are the rules under which children are admitted to the school: they set the age group for admission, the number of pupils who can be admitted and the criteria that will apply if more children apply than there are places for – these are known as over-subscription criteria. These criteria are set by the relevant admission authority and must be in accordance with the School Admissions Code.

All academy trusts are admission authorities and responsible for setting the admission arrangements for the mainstream authorities they run.

Checklist

School Admissions Code

▶ The admission authority must determine the admission arrangements annually.

▶ Admission criteria apply to the usual point of entry to the children – e.g. in an 11–16 school this will be Year 7. There must be admission arrangements for every relevant age group – i.e. if the school also has a sixth form then there will need to be two sets of admission arrangements, one for Year 7 and for Year 12. All-through schools which may have three points of entry (Reception, Year 7 and Year 12). Pupils will be admitted in September (i.e. the beginning of the academic year).

▶ Admission authorities must determine the planned admission number (PAN). This is the number of children who are to be admitted to the particular year group. The PAN is usually related to the overall capacity of the buildings the school is based in.

▶ Over-subscription criteria must be reasonable, clear, objective, procedurally fair, and comply with all relevant legislation, including equalities legislation.

▶ Admission arrangements must be consulted on every seven years whether they have been amended or not.

▷ Admission criteria must be objective and may not consider individual pupil characteristics. The exception to this is if the funding agreement or supplementary funding agreement has designated the school: to have a religious character, to be selective or partially selective or to be a single sex school.

▷ Admission criteria must be published in February for admissions the following September, i.e. in February 2019 for admissions in September 2020.

▷ Consultation – with few exceptions changes to the admission arrangements must be consulted on. Admission authorities can increase the PAN without consultation. The Schools Admissions Code sets out who must be consulted.

▷ Academy admission arrangements are included in the LA's composite admissions prospectus.

▷ Parents apply for places on the LA common admission form.

▷ Consultation on admission arrangements must allow a six-week period for comment and must take place between 1 October and 31 January for publication of final arrangements by 28 February.

▷ Finalised admission arrangements must be published by 28 February for admissions in the September of the following year (i.e. February 2019 for admission in September 2020).

▷ If fewer pupils apply than there are places, then all pupils must be admitted.

▷ If the admission authority is proposing to decrease its PAN, then it must consult.

▷ Unless schools have been formally designated as being selective, single sex or are schools with a religious character, pupil or parental characteristics must play no part in the admission arrangements.

▷ Special schools have different admission arrangements. Pupils will generally only be admitted to a special school if they have an Education Health and Care Plan (EHCP). The local authority in which the pupil resides is responsible for putting in place an EHCP and this will usually name the school they will attend. If a school is named on an EHCP then it must admit the child.

▷ Alternative provision academies are also different because they do not take children at a set time of the year. AP academies cater for children who have been permanently excluded from other schools or who have under a special arrangement with the pupil's home school for a short period of time to improve behaviour.

▷ Academy trusts are required by their funding agreements to act in accordance with the School Admission Code. The Secretary of the State has the power to vary this requirement, but it is only used in exceptional circumstances.

Mainstream academies

▷ The SoD must specify who is responsible for setting admission arrangements, operational staff, a trustee committee, or in MATs if this is delegated to the academy committee.

▷ Ensure those responsible for determining admission arrangement have received appropriate training and understand the requirements of the School Admission Code.

▷ Determine academy admission arrangements in accordance with the School Admission Code.

▷ Admission authorities must determine applications solely based on the over-subscription criteria.

▷ Academy trusts must have arrangements in place to hear any appeals against non-admission. These must be organised in line with the Schools Admissions Appeals Code.

▷ Website – determined admission arrangements must be published on the website of the individual academy. They must remain on the website for the whole year.

Procedure

▷ The SoD is reviewed and approved annually at a properly convened and quorate trustees' meeting – responsibility for determining admission arrangements must be included on the SoD.

▷ Those in the trust with delegated authority to determine admission arrangements must arrange to do so in accordance with the timescales and guidance in the Code.

▷ Ensure any changes to admission arrangements are publicised and properly consulted on.

▷ Publish determined admission arrangements in line with statutory deadlines on the website of individual academies.

▷ Allocate places at academies in line with admission arrangements.

▷ Ensure an independent appeals panel is in place to hear any appeals against non-admission.

Notes

▷ It is important that academy trusts adhere to the School Admissions Code and particularly ensure that their admission arrangements meet the 'reasonable, clear, objective and procedurally fair' stipulation in the Code. Objections against admission arrangements can be made to the Schools Adjudicator and annually the Adjudicator reports that the majority of complaints upheld are against own admission authorities (such as academy trusts) and that the failure to observe the 'reasonable… fair' stipulation is the biggest reason for objections being upheld.

▶ Where the academy trust is required to consult about its admission arrangements it should ensure that it does so in a full and comprehensive manner.

More information

▶ School Admissions Code: www.gov.uk/government/publications/school-admissions-code—2

▶ School Admission Regulations 2012: www.legislation.gov.uk/uksi/2012/8/made

▶ School Admission Appeal Code: www.gov.uk/government/publications/school-admissions-appeals-code

▶ School Admissions (Appeal Arrangements) (England) Regulations 2012: www.legislation.gov.uk/uksi/2012/9/made

Agreement to short notice

Introduction

In most cases members of academy trusts as private companies can agree to accept shorter notice of a meeting than that prescribed in the Companies Act.

Academy trusts need to check their articles of association as to the rules for calling short notice meetings. The current model articles allow for short notice meeting if it is agreed by a majority in number of members having a right to attend and vote and together representing not less than 90% of the total voting rights at that meeting. Some earlier versions of the articles have different provisions.

It is recommended that agreements to short notice are in writing and kept with the minutes of the meeting.

Even where members have agreed to a short notice meeting, they are not required to attend in person and can send a proxy.

Short notice should be used sparingly.

Checklist

▶ Check that the requisite number of members has agreed to a short notice meeting.

Procedure

▶ The company secretary/clerk should circulate an agreement to short notice along with a copy of the notice of meeting and requests signature and return.

Filing requirements

None.

Analyse School Performance

Introduction

Analyse School Performance (ASP) is the DfE's online system for providing schools with in-depth analysis of their KS1, KS2, KS4 and KS5 results. It is only available to those with authorised log-ins to the site. Operational staff can use the site to look at data at individual pupil level. Trustees can be given access to the site and look at data at school level.

It allows users to explore data in more detail according to pupil characteristics or compare outcomes for different pupil groups. It contains a range of downloadable reports; at secondary level these are by subject. It also has attendance and exclusion information over a three-year period.

Finally, there is an option to download the Ofsted inspection data summary report (IDSR). This resource will be used by Ofsted when inspecting a school and is therefore essential reading for those governing. It should be read alongside the information provided through ASP.

Checklist

▶ Some trustees should have access to the ASP site.

Procedure

▶ Trustees should ask the senior executive leader to ensure some of their number are provided with governor-level access to the site.

Annual general meeting

Introduction

Under the CA2006 private companies, such as academy trusts, do not need to hold an annual general meeting (AGM) unless their articles of association require them to.

The model articles of association for academy trusts do include this provision; although it is given as an 'optional' article it is the recommendation of the DfE that it is adopted.

Articles generally require that trusts hold their first AGM within 18 months of incorporation and thereafter no more than 15 months should elapse between one AGM and another.

The normal or 'ordinary' business of the AGM is to receive the most recent accounts.

Checklist

▷ An AGM shall be held in each academy financial year and not more than 15 months later than the previous meeting.

▷ Are any member-appointed trustees coming to the end of their terms of office – will reappointment or new appointments be required on the agenda?

▷ Check whether any members need to be appointed.

▷ Check whether there are any validly proposed special resolutions which need to be included in the notice.

▷ Are the auditors to be reappointed or are new auditors being appointed requiring special notice.

▷ The remuneration of the auditors must be fixed by the members or in such manner as they shall approve.

▷ Consider whether there is any other business to be put before the members (e.g. changes to the articles of association, name of the trust or removal of directors).

▷ Ensure all involved are clear about who will chair the meeting or how the chair will be appointed.

Procedure

▷ Convene a trustees'/directors' meeting to recommend appropriate resolution(s) to members and to convene the AGM. Ensure a valid quorum present.

▷ Only the trustees/directors may validly convene an AGM (members only have the power to call general meetings). The directors should formally convene the meeting and approve the contents of the notice and accompanying documents.

▷ Issue notice signed by a director or the company secretary convening the AGM of the academy trust on 14 clear days notice for members to consider resolutions.

▷ Given notice according to the provisions of the articles, this may be hard copy or electronically or a mixture of both.

▷ A copy of the notice should be sent to non-member trustees and the company's auditors.

▷ Hold AGM. Ensure valid quorum is present.

▷ If necessary, appoint a chair – current model articles allow for the members present to appoint a chair from among their number, some previous versions of the articles stipulate the meeting will be chaired by the chair of the trustee board.

▷ Resolutions put to the vote either by show or hand or by poll and to be passed by appropriate majority (ordinary resolutions by 50% majority, special resolutions by 75%).

▷ Ensure minutes of AGM are prepared as soon as possible.

Filing requirements

▷ Copies of any special resolutions and those order resolutions where notification required.

▷ Any appropriate forms relating to non-reappointment of directors or auditors.

Notes

▷ Legally, AGMs need only be open to members and directors; however, as academy trusts are publicly funded it is worth considering whether the opportunity ought to be given to other stakeholders to attend and ask questions.

Annual general meeting – good practice

Introduction

While the AGM requirement stems from the academy trust's position as a corporate company the trust should bear in mind that as publicly funded charitable companies the Nolan principles of accountability and openness apply, and they may wish to open the AGM up to a wider group of stakeholders, e.g. parents.

Venue size will be dependent on whether the directors/members choose to open the meeting to those not otherwise entitled to attend.

Checklist

Before the meeting

▶ A suitable venue needs to be arranged for the AGM – trustees as well as members are entitled to attend so the venue needs to have enough capacity to accommodate them comfortably as well.

▶ Confirm the date of the meeting with the board, advisers and all others required or entitled to attend as soon as possible.

AGM notice – explanatory notes

▶ While the core content of an AGM notice is set out in the CA2006 it is good practice to provide additional information to clarify procedure or anticipate questions. This should include:

▷ a statement of corporate/foundation members' rights to appoint one or more proxies;
▷ instructions on how and when the proxy appointment should be returned and a statement that the return of a proxy form does not prevent the member from attending in person;
▷ if relevant, that the chairman intends to call a poll on any or all resolutions; and
▷ an explanation of how the voting will take place at the meeting.

Proxies

- A proxy appointment should provide information on how to appoint a person or persons, other than the chair as proxy – most academy trust articles of association include rules about the appointment of proxies and wording for declarations.

- Before the meeting, ensure the chair is aware of how many, if any, proxies there are and specifically where the chair has been appointed as proxy.

Preparing the chair of the trust

- Brief the chair on the main provisions in the articles governing the organisation and procedure of the meeting, voting procedures and their role and powers of the meeting.

- If required, prepare a script for the chair and a pack with potential questions and answers – this might be of particular need if the meeting has been opened to non-members or there is a particularly controversial resolution.

- Ensure that the chairs of any trustee committees, AO and CFO are present and briefed.

- At the meeting the following documents might be useful:

  - AGM notice and form of proxy;
  - annual reports and accounts;
  - the chair's script (if there is one);
  - copies of presentations;
  - questions and answers briefing; and
  - the articles of association.

Chair of the meeting

- Check the articles to confirm who is entitled to chair the meeting.

- Allow adequate time to allow for questions from the floor.

- Where items of business require resolutions there should be separate resolutions for different items of business.

Voting

- If a poll is likely then the company secretary/clerk should ensure poll cards are available.

- Before any resolution is put to the vote the chair should explain its effect and purpose and if necessary elaborate upon any information issued in explanatory notes circulated with the notice. Members/trustees may also be invited to speak.

- The chair should indicate how many proxies are held.

- If a poll is taken then the number of votes, for against and abstentions, should be announced.

After the meeting

▶ Following the meeting the company secretary/clerk is responsible for ensuring that all minutes, forms and resolutions are prepared and signed and appropriately filed.

Minutes and registers

▶ Prepare the minutes of the meeting.

▶ Once agreed, the minutes should be signed by the chair.

▶ If appropriate, update the registers of directors, secretaries, members charges or debenture holders.

Filing requirements

▶ Will depend on the business of the meeting. There may be requirements to file with Companies House.

Annual trustees' report

Introduction

Trustees must prepare an annual trustees' report.

The report accompanies the annual accounts and provides a wider commentary of the strategic objectives and the trustee board's performance during the year reported on. The report can and should 'add value' to the financial data provided by the accounts – i.e. it should provide more detail about the company's activities.

The trustee board as a whole is responsible for the contents of the report and for ensuring those contents include all the relevant material required by law and applicable accounting and reporting standards.

The accounting and reporting standards for charities recognise that numbers are not, of themselves, enough to show the overall picture of a charity's activities and its end-of-year position. Further, the figures alone cannot tell the story of the public benefit that has been provided and the good the charity is doing – whereas an imaginative trustees' report certainly can.

The ESFA adapts the Charity SORP to take account of academy trusts' responsibilities as publicly funded entities. Academy trusts must take account of the Academies Accounts Direction, which also requires a governance statement to be included as an additional and distinct part of the annual return.

Checklist

▶ Ensure the report complies with all applicable legislation and with the sector-specific SORP for academy trusts.

Public benefit

▶ The report must include:

▷ a report of the activities undertaken by the charity to further its charitable purposes for the public benefit; and

▷ a statement by the trustees as to whether they have complied with their duty to have regard to the Charity Commission's guidance on public benefit.

Governance statement

▶ As central government public sector bodies, academy trusts are required to provide assurance that they are appropriately managed and are controlling the resources for which they are responsible. The governance statement must include the following sections:

▷ the 'scope of responsibility' section within the governance statement is generic in nature and therefore applicable to all academy trusts – unless the trust has not appointed the senior executive leader as AO;

▷ governance – a brief description of the governance framework of the academy trust is required, including information about the committee structure, attendance records. If this information has been covered elsewhere it need not be included twice;

▷ a review of value for money – a standard declaration acknowledging the AO's responsibility for ensuring value for money and examples of how the trust has achieved this;

▷ a description of the purpose of the system of internal control and as statement by the trustees confirming that the system of internal control has been in place for the year;

▷ the capacity to handle risk – description of how risk management fits with the leadership of the trust and how the trustee board has considered and reviewed the risks and what mitigation measures have been taken. Also requires a statement about the effectiveness of ongoing risk management measures;

▷ a description of the key elements of the risk and control framework including a description of the delivery of an internal audit/internal checking/oversight function;

▷ details of the extent of the review of effectiveness of the system of internal control and identify the areas that have informed the review; and

▷ a statement on regularity, propriety and compliance – required by the Academies Accounts Direction because the academy trust is publicly funded. This must be signed by the accounting officer. In effect a statement confirming that funds have been used in accordance with legislation, guidance and that mechanisms are in place to ensure funds cannot be used improperly.

Procedure

▶ Prepare the report in accordance with the legislative requirements and the Academies Accounts Direction.

▶ Arrange approval by the trustee board.

▶ Ensure the trustees authorise the relevant signatory.

▶ Minute the approval of the report and the authorisation of the signatory.

▶ Arrange the filing of the report with the annual accounts, with all relevant regulators.

▶ Ensure the accounts are published on the website by 31 January.

Filing requirements

▶ The trustees' annual report with the accounts must be filed with the ESFA by 31 December and Companies House (within nine months of the end of the academy trust's financial year).

▶ Academy trusts must publish accounts on their website by 31 January following the end of their financial year.

Notes

▶ The trustees' report is an opportunity to set out what the academy trust has achieved and how.

▶ Governance statement – there is an expectation that the trustees will have reviewed the effectiveness of the board – in new trusts this is a requirement. There are several tools the board can use to do this. The Charity Governance Code (see page 80) recommends that the board reviews its own practice annually and seeks an external review every three years.

▶ Value for money – AOs should set out how value for money has been achieved not just by the trust but on behalf of the taxpayer. It should demonstrate how the trust continuously improves both the educational and wider societal outcomes for acknowledging the accounting officer's responsibility for value for money. It should include short examples.

Articles of association – adoption or change

Introduction

The articles of association are the rules governing the company's internal affairs. The DfE provides model articles for adoption by academy trusts. There are separate models provided for church trusts and UTCs.

Alteration of any regulation or adoption of new articles requires a special resolution of the members in a general meeting.

The main reasons academy trusts amend their articles are:

▶ when a SAT becomes a MAT; and

▶ when MATs update their articles to adopt provisions in the DfE model articles.

Academy trusts need the approval of the Secretary of State (via the ESFA) to change their articles of association. In certain circumstances, usually church trusts, they may also need the approval of the Charity Commission.

Checklist

▶ Consider whether amendment can be undertaken by amending existing clauses, by the adoption of new clauses in addition to or in substitution of existing clauses or by the adoption of a complete new set of articles (i.e. the latest DfE model).

▶ Check which bodies (e.g. Charity Commission/ESFA) also need to approve any changes to the articles.

▶ Consider the implications of permission to change being refused.

Procedure

▶ Convene a trustees' meeting to consider and recommend resolutions to members and to convene a general meeting or circulate a written resolution if appropriate.

▶ Obtain any required prior regulatory consents; at the very least it is worth having a conversation with the Regional Schools Commissioner's (RSC's) office to assess the likelihood of approval.

▶ Issue a notice, signed by a trustee or company secretary convening a general meeting, giving 14 clear days' notice, or circulate written resolution for members to consider special resolution to amend the articles.

▶ As a special resolution the resolution must include the full text of the proposed changes.

▶ If the meeting is to be convened at short notice the company secretary/clerk should arrange for the short notice agreement to be signed by each of the members.

▶ Hold a general meeting and ensure that it is quorate. Resolutions put to the vote either by show of hands or by poll and must be passed by the requisite majority (special resolutions required 75% majority).

▶ If the resolution is circulated by means of a written resolution the resolution must receive approval of the holders of at least 75% of the members entitled to vote within 28 days of the circulation date of the resolution (see page 253).

Filing requirements

▶ Signed copy of the special resolution and amended articles must be filed with Companies House within 15 days.

▶ If the changes required prior regulatory consent this must also be included.

▶ If the objects have been altered, form CC04 (Statement of company's objects) is also required.

Notes

▶ The DfE publishes model articles for all variations of SATs and MATs; it is unlikely to approve any clauses that vary significantly from these models.

▶ The DfE is likely to look favourably where an existing trust wants to amend its articles to adopt the latest version of the model articles.

Articles of association – general

Introduction

An academy trust's articles of association are its governing document. The DfE provides a range of model articles of association, depending on the categories of academies within the trust. Academy trusts are expected to adopt these model articles without any significant variation.

The model articles have changed over time, so it is always necessary to check the precise wording of the particular trust.

Checklist

▷ The Academy trust's articles must be approved by the DfE.

Effect and impact

▷ The academy trust's articles take effect from the date of incorporation.

▷ All members of the company are bound by the articles.

▷ The directors/trustees have a legal duty to:

  ▷ act in accordance with the articles; and
  ▷ only exercise their powers (including powers set out in the articles) for the purposes which the powers are conferred.

Decisions

▷ In carrying out or authorising any decision/action by the academy trust, as well as bearing in mind their general responsibilities under charity and company law as directors and trustees, trustees must satisfy themselves that:

  ▷ the decision is one that they/the trust is entitled to make and it is not prevented/restricted by the articles;
  ▷ the trustees do have the authority under the articles to exercise the power; and
  ▷ the trustees are exercising the power for the purpose for which it was conferred by the articles.

Changes to the articles of association

▶ The academy trust must get the consent of the DfE before making changes to its articles of association.

Members' rights

▶ The articles will set out details of rights of members, but some rights are enshrined in the CA2006 and cannot be overridden by articles of association. These are the right to:

▷ receive copies of the annual accounts and trustees' report;

▷ appoint a proxy of the member's own choice to attend and vote at general meetings of the members on behalf of the appointer; and

▷ give (or withhold) consent to the variation of the rights of the membership class to which the member belongs.

Filing requirements

▶ The academy trust's original articles are filed at Companies House with its incorporation documents.

▶ All subsequent amendments to the articles must also be filed along with the accompanying special resolution under which such changes were brought into effect. The DfE's consent will be required to changes to the articles.

Notes

▶ The DfE produces model articles of association which all academy trusts are expected to adopt. The models have been amended several times and it is open to existing trusts to seek to adopt the most recent version. The DfE is likely to look favourably on such requests.

More information

▶ Academy Governance Checklists: Articles of association – adoption or change.

Audit Committee

Introduction

All academy trusts are required by the AFH 2018 section 2.9.1 to have an audit committee.

The purpose of the audit committee is to provide assurance to the board over the suitability of, and compliance with, its financial systems and operational controls, and to ensure that risks are being adequately identified and managed.

Where the trust has annual income of more than £50 million it must have a separate audit committee. Trusts with income of less than £50 million can combine the audit committee with the finance committee. Employees should not sit on the audit committee. Where there is a combined finance and audit committee and employees do sit on the finance committee, they should not sit as committee members when it is acting as the audit committee.

Non-trustees can be appointed by the trustees to the audit committee providing that the majority of any members of the committee are trustees. No vote of the audit committee will be valid unless the majority of its members present and voting are trustees.

Checklist

▷ Articles require that the membership and remit of committees is considered annually by trustees. Decision-making powers must be recorded in the SoD.

▷ Check that the trustee board has established an audit committee. Some smaller trusts operate without other committees, but they must still establish an audit committee.

▷ Check whether the annual income is more than £50 million – if so, a separate audit committee must be established.

▷ Ensure the constitution of the committee meets the requirements of the articles and AFH 2018.

▷ Ensure the audit committee has a plan for the year which will cover consideration of financial controls and risks, including in MATs at individual academies within the trust.

▷ Ensure that oversight includes checking that the information submitted to DfE/ESFA relating to the funding of the trust is accurate.

▷ Does the SoD accurately record decision-making powers delegated to the finance/audit committee?

Procedure

▷ Trustees must approve the membership, terms of reference and decision-making powers of the audit committee annually. This is usually done at the first full meeting of the board of trustees in the autumn term.

▷ Ensure the SoD is updated and published on the trust website.

▷ The audit committee should agree a programme of work to ensure it fulfils the requirements of the AFH 2018.

Notes

▷ The AFH 2018 states that employees should not be members of the audit committee, but in any case this would not be good practice. Relevant employees, e.g. CFO and AO, should be expected to attend, provide information and participate in discussion but not be formal members of the committee.

Auditors – appointment to a private company

Introduction

Academy trusts are required by the CA2006, their funding agreement and the AFH to appoint independent auditors.

The auditor must hold a current audit-practising certificate issued by a recognised supervisory body and be completely independent of the trust. The audit should be carried out in accordance with International Standards on Auditing. The audit must certify that academy trusts' annual accounts present a true and fair view of the trust's financial performance and position.

Checklist

▶ Have qualified auditors been appointed in writing?

▶ Ensure the letter of engagement stipulates how the auditors can be removed.

▶ Other than for the first set of accounts when the trustees may appoint, it is the responsibility of the members to appoint the auditors.

Procedure

▶ Convene a trustees' meeting to appoint the auditors (first accounts only).

▶ Convene a members' meeting to appoint auditors, or arrange a written resolution of members.

Filing requirements

None.

Auditors – removal

Introduction

The members of an academy trust may remove the auditors from office by ordinary resolution. In practice this is an unusual occurrence and the trustees would normally invite the auditors to resign or propose that the auditors are not reappointed at a general meeting at which accounts are laid.

The AFH 2018 requires that the letter of engagement to auditors sets out the terms in which the auditors may be removed. Removal of the auditor before the end of the term of office is a serious matter and usually signifies serious problems with the charity.

If the trustees are considering proposing the removal of the auditors, they should seek professional advice before doing so.

Checklist

▶ Decision must be made at a general meeting. Auditors cannot be removed by written resolution.

▶ Special notice, i.e. notice of the proposed resolution must be given at least 28 days before the meeting at which the resolution to remove an auditor is to be heard.

▶ A copy of the special notice must be sent to the auditor whose removal is proposed.

▶ The auditor may make written representations concerning their removal and request that this is either sent to members or, if time will not allow, read out at the meeting.

▶ On removal, notice of that removal must be filed at Companies House within 14 days.

Procedure

▶ Special notice is given by a trustee to the company.

▷ Convene a trustees' meeting to recommend resolution to members and convene a general meeting. Ensure valid quorum is present.

▷ Copy of the special notice is sent to the auditor.

▷ Issue notice, signed by director or company secretary, convening general meeting with 14 clear days' notice for members to consider.

▷ Ordinary resolution to remove auditor.

▷ If the meeting is to be convened at short notice the company secretary/clerk should arrange for agreement to short notice to be signed by the members.

▷ Representation of auditors circulated with notice or separately. If not circulated read auditors' representation to the meeting.

▷ Hold general meeting. Ensure quorum is present. Resolutions put to vote either by show of hands or poll and to be passed by appropriate majority (ordinary resolution by 50% majority).

▷ If removal approved, notify the ESFA immediately and Companies House within 14 days.

Filing requirements

▷ Form AA03 Companies House within 14 days.

▷ ESFA immediately.

Notes

▷ Removal of auditors before the expiry of their term of office should only be considered in exceptional circumstances. Where any academy trust is considering this step, it is advisable to contact the ESFA at the earliest opportunity.

Auditors – resignation

Introduction

Auditors may resign from office by giving notice in writing to the registered office of the academy trust.

Academy trusts are required to appoint auditors in writing and the letter of engagement must include a requirement for auditors to provide written reasons for their resignation to the trust within 14 days of resigning.

Where auditors resign, they may provide a statement of any matters they consider should be brought to the attention of members or, if there are no such circumstances, a statement to that effect.

Checklist

▷ Auditors' resignation is received at the registered office.

▷ Written reasons for resignation received at registered office within 14 days of resignation.

▷ The trust must circulate the statement to members within 14 days of receipt unless a court order has been sought.

▷ The trust must notify the ESFA of the resignation immediately and copy any statement provided by the auditors.

▷ If a court order is not obtained then the trust must circulate the statement to members within 14 days of the court's decision and notify the auditors.

▷ Unless notice of an application for a court order is received within 21 days the auditors must file a copy of their statement with Companies House within 28 days of the original notice of resignation.

Procedure

▷ Circulate statement of circumstances to members, unless a court order has been applied for. If court order has been applied for, notify auditor within 21 days of original notice being received.

▶ Notify the ESFA immediately of resignation. Provide a copy of the statement issued by the auditors.

Filing requirements

▶ Copy of auditors' resignation letter within 14 days at Companies House.

▶ Immediate notification to the ESFA of the resignation and a copy of the resignation statement from the auditors as soon as received.

▶ Auditors to file statement of circumstances after 21 days but before 28 days unless court application made.

▶ If court upholds application, copy of that decision to be circulated to members.

▶ If application not upheld, statement to be circulated to members within 14 days and notify auditors who must file their statement at Companies House within the next seven days.

Bank account

Introduction

All academy trusts must have a bank account. In MATs it is a matter for the trustee board whether there is just one MAT central bank account or whether individual academies can have their own accounts.

The trustees have ultimate responsibility for the charity's banking arrangements and should make decisions about opening the bank account and any decision to move accounts.

While the trustees will delegate the day-to-day operation of the bank accounts to the senior executive leader and trust staff, they should have mechanisms in place to assure themselves that there are adequate controls in place. This is set out in Charity Commission Guidance and is a requirement of the AFH 2018.

Banks will have standard forms/mandates for academy trusts to complete to open, or switch, bank accounts. Many banks have specialist education teams.

The AFH places particular responsibilities on the accounting officer (see page 13) to have appropriate oversight of financial transactions, by ensuring that bank accounts, financial systems and financial records are operated by more than one person.

All academy trusts are required by the AFH to have a written scheme of delegation of financial powers.

Checklist

▷ Ensure there is an approved written scheme of delegation of financial powers that clearly sets out the financial limits of authority for all staff.

▷ Ensure that appropriate financial controls are in place to ensure that the bank account cannot be operated by a single person.

▷ Review the authorised signatories and authority levels annually.

Notes

▷ MATs will need to consider whether to have a single bank account or allow their academies to have separate accounts.

▷ In a letter to auditors in 2018, Lord Agnew, the Parliamentary under Secretary of State for the School System (with responsibility for academies), indicated that a single bank account was his preferred option. His letter suggested that in looking at MAT accounts auditors should look at whether they 'have a central bank account that simplifies bank reconciliations'.

Board evaluations

Introduction

It is considered good governance best practice for the board to monitor and evaluate its own effectiveness. The DfE's *Governance Handbook* states that the board should have processes in place for regular self-evaluation, including of individual's contribution to the board.

A board evaluation should review all aspects of a board's effectiveness, in particular:

▶ the composition of the board: does it have a good balance of skills, experience and knowledge among its trustees; and

▶ committee structure: is this working effectively to ensure the board can exercise proper strategic oversight and ensure compliance with statutory requirements. In a MAT this will also encompass the arrangements at academy committee level.

Checklist

The Charity Governance Code states:

▶ 'The board reviews its own performance and that of individual trustees, including the chair. This happens every year, with an external evaluation every three years. Such evaluation typically considers the board's balance of skills, experience and knowledge, its diversity in the widest sense, how the board works together and other factors relevant to its effectiveness... The board explains how the charity reviews or evaluates the board in the governance statement in the trustees' annual report.'

▶ Academy trusts must also follow the instructions in the Academies Accounts Direction which stipulates that academy trusts in their first year, must review the effectiveness of their governance arrangements and other trusts should, as a matter of best practice, do so annually. In the Governance Statement required by the Academies Accounts Direction trusts should set out the outcomes, actions and impact of any review. If the academy trust has not undertaken a review during the year then they should set out when they intend to do so.

▷ It is generally considered best practice for the board to review its own effectiveness annually and every three years to have an external review.

▷ All prospective trustees should be asked to fill in a skills audit, setting out their skills, experience, aptitudes and knowledge. The governance professional should maintain an overarching matrix of the board's skills, experience and knowledge. This should be used to recruit new trustees (see page 297).

▷ There are a range of tools available to enable boards to conduct a review and a range of organisations and individuals who could conduct an external review.

▷ The DfE's *Governance Handbook* states that governing boards have three core functions:

  ▷ ensuring clarity of vision, ethos and strategic direction;
  ▷ holding executive leaders to account for the educational performance of the organisation and its pupils, and the performance management of staff; and
  ▷ overseeing the financial performance of the organisation and making sure its money is well spent.

▷ Any review of the trustee board should consider how effectively it is fulfilling these functions.

Procedure

▷ The trustee board needs to determine whether the review will be self-conducted or an external review.

Internal review

▷ Set a date for the review – allow enough time for a thorough review – it is better not to tack this on to other board business.

▷ Decide who will lead the board review – this could be the chair, vice chair or the clerk/governance professional.

▷ Agree who besides trustees will be asked to contribute to the review – i.e. which members of staff and in MATs how will you involve those sitting on academy committees.

▷ Agree what tools you will use to conduct the review – this could be delegated to the person leading the review.

▷ Agenda – set out an agenda for the day as you would for any other meeting – the review needs to be structured so cover all the ground you want to.

▷ Engage – a review will only be useful if all trustees commit to it.

▷ Notes – ensure someone is taking notes of the discussion – or if you are using post-it notes/flip charts that these are collected up afterwards.

▷ Action – trustees should agree what action will be taken as a result of the review.

▷ Review – trustees should monitor progress on agreed actions.

External review

▷ Trustees should formally approve the scope and budget for the review.

▷ The person/organisation contracted to undertake the review should be independent of the trust.

▷ Ensure the person contracted to undertake the review understands academy trust/MAT governance.

▷ Delegate the organisation of a review to the chair/vice chair.

▷ Set a date for the review – allow enough time on the day for the review and ensure as many as trustees as possible (preferably all) can attend.

▷ Pre-meeting work – most external reviews involve some form of pre-meeting anonymous questionnaire to fill in. All trustees should be required to fill this in, even if they can't attend the actual review.

▷ The questionnaire can be used to determine which areas of board practice should be the focus of the review day.

▷ Report – ensure the trustees receive a full report of the findings of the review.

▷ Action – trustees should agree what action you will take as a result of the review.

▷ Review – trustees should monitor their progress against agreed actions.

▷ Whether the review is internal or external it needs to assess both the effectiveness of the trustee board as unit and the contributions individuals are making. Some key areas a board review may want to consider are:

  ▷ the diversity (in its widest sense) of the trustee board – the range of skills, experience and knowledge and how these fit with the challenges facing the trust;
  ▷ over time the skills, experience and knowledge the trustee board requires may well change – this will be the case in a MAT;
  ▷ does the trustee board effectively lead the organisation to meet its strategic aims?

▷ How well does the trustee board work as a unit?

▷ Relationships – are the key relationships within the trust working well, i.e. chair/senior executive lead, chair/vice chair, chair/governance professional, trustee board and those at academy level?

▷ How effectively do individual trustees contribute?

▷ Are the board structures (i.e. committees) effective?

▷ In MATs how effective are academy committees and how effectively do they support the strategic aims of the board?

▷ Is the board supported by high-quality data and reports? Does the board receive the right information to make good decisions?

▷ Are delegated authorities set at the right level to enable effective decision making?

▷ How good is the standard of discussion around the board table?

▷ Is the board supported by an effective governance professional?

▷ How does the board communicate, consult and listen to stakeholders (pupils, parents and staff)?

This list is not exhaustive, or prescriptive; boards in conjunction with any facilitator will need to ensure any review is bespoke to its needs.

More information

▷ Tools for use for board review:

▷ 20 Questions – Twenty Key Questions for the Governing Board to ask itself: www.nga.org.uk/About-Us/APPG/Home/Twenty-Questions-(1).aspx

▷ 21 Questions – Twenty-one Questions for Multi-academy Trusts: www.nga.org.uk/About-Us/APPG/Home/21Questions.aspx

▷ National Governance Association self-evaluation tools: www.nga.org.uk/ConsultancyandTraining/Online-evaluation-tools.aspx

▷ ICSA: Academy School Governance Maturity Matrix: www.icsa.org.uk/knowledge/resources/guidance-notes

▷ ICSA: Multi-Academy Trust Governance – Board Effectiveness: www.icsa.org.uk/knowledge/resources/guidance-notes

▷ DfE Competency Framework for Governance: www.gov.uk/government/publications/governance-handbook

▷ NCVO – Governance Wheel.

External reviews

Explanation

The DfE's website contains some information about external reviews, including how to commission them, what they might cover and who might conduct them. The DfE particularly refers to National Leaders of Governance (NLGs) and National Leaders of Education (NLE), but both NLGs and NLEs were recruited to carry out an entirely different role and not all will have the requisite skills/experience to carry out a review: www.gov.uk/guidance/reviews-of-school-governance

It is for the academy trustee board to make the final decision about who to contract to undertake the review. The key consideration for any trust is ensuring they contract with someone who has both knowledge of the academy trust sector and an understanding of the overarching principles of good governance (see page 162). As with any contract it is wise to seek testimonials of previous work undertaken.

More information

▶ National Governance Association: www.nga.org.uk/ ConsultancyandTraining/Multi-academy-trusts.aspx

▶ *Academy Governance Handbook*, Chapter 10.

Board skills audit and register

Introduction

In order to be effective, the trustee board needs to recruit trustees with a range of skills, experience and knowledge.

The AFH 2018 says that 'The board should identify the skills and experience that it needs, and address any gaps through recruitment, and/ or induction, training and other development activities'. It makes clear that in MATs this should be extended to those sitting on ACs, although the skills required will be dependent on what is delegated to AC level.

Trusts should use a skills audit to indicate the range of skills/experience needed on the trustee board. Individual trustees should be asked to fill in the skills audit so that their skills/experiences can be mapped against the trust's requirements. Not every member of the trustee board will have every skill identified as necessary to govern the trust, the important thing is that the board encompasses these skills. The governance professional should maintain a register of the skills of the whole board so that gaps can be readily identified. This register can then be used for when there is a vacancy on the trustee board to fill any skills gaps and to identify the development needs of the board.

Prospective trustees should be asked to fill in the skills audit as part of the recruitment process. Even where the position being recruited to is via election this is good practice.

There is a range of skills audit tools available for trustee boards to use.

Skills audits include a considerable element of self-assessment, so it is important that there is also a box which asks for evidence to back up the rating.

Checklist

▶ Develop a skills audit for your academy trustee board.

▶ Everyone on the board should fill in the skills audit.

▶ The governance professional should amalgamate the responses from each trustee into a matrix to enable an assessment.

▶ Skills audit should be used to identify gaps and recruit new trustees.

▶ All prospective trustees should be required to fill in the skills audit.

▶ Review the skills audit annually, especially if the organisation is undergoing significant change.

Tools

▶ There is a range of tools available to help trustee boards:

▷ DfE Competency Framework for Governance (NB this is very detailed and is better used to develop a skills audit than to be used wholesale with trustees/prospective trustees): www.gov.uk/government/publications/governance-handbook

▷ NGA Skills audit tool – this has been developed around the six features of effective governance in the DfE's Competency Framework: www.nga.org.uk/Guidance/Workings-Of-The-Governing-Body/Governance-Tools/Skills-Audit.aspx

More information

▶ *Academy Governance Handbook*, Chapter 10.

Budget forecast return

Introduction

There are two budget forecast returns: the budget forecast return (BFR) and the budget forecast return outturn (BFRO). All established academy trusts are required to submit these returns to the ESFA.

The BFR collects three-year forecast data. The ESFA uses this data to provide HM Treasury with forecasts. It is also used by the ESFA to assess the health of the academies sector and check that trusts are planning strategically. The BFR is an online return. It is usually opened at the beginning of June each year and trusts must submit returns by the end of July.

The BFRO collects outturn information, which again is used to provide information to HM Treasury. The return usually has to be submitted by May.

The ESFA provides guidance each year for academy trusts on how to complete the return.

Checklist

▷ Consider who needs to approve the BFR.

▷ Ensure the BFR is submitted within set timescales.

▷ Ensure the BFRO is submitted on time.

Procedures

▷ Convene a meeting of the trustees, or relevant committee, to approve the BFR.

Notes

▷ While the finance staff of the trust will be responsible for submitting the BFR returns to the ESFA, the trustees must take an interest in the three-year budget forecast return. Trustees have overall responsibility for the financial health of the organisation and, therefore, it is vital that they also receive forecasts of the trust's future financial position. If the trust is facing financial difficulties these need to be planned for and addressed at the earliest opportunity.

More information

▶ DfE website – BFR pages: www.gov.uk/guidance/academies-budget-forecast-return

▶ *Academy Governance Handbook*, Chapter 12.

Capital funding – general

Introduction

Capital funding is money provided by the DfE for spending on school buildings and major items such as IT equipment. It cannot be spent on day-to-day running costs of the school or routine maintenance. There are a range of separate capital grants currently provided to academy trusts.

Trustees are responsible for the upkeep of the premises. They have duties as employers under the Health and Safety at Work Act to ensure that the premises are safe. In addition, the charitable objects of academy trusts are about educational outcomes, where buildings and classroom facilities are poor; this is not likely to be conducive to learning.

Almost all school buildings contain asbestos and trustees must ensure that there is an appropriate plan in place for managing this.

Trustees should have a clear and complete picture of the estate they are managing and the priorities for improvement and maintenance. Trustees will need to keep a closer eye on any significant capital projects.

Capital grants available from the ESFA

Devolved formula capital

▷ This is paid to every academy. As its name implies, it is calculated on a formulaic basis. All schools receive a lump sum amount – currently £4,000 per school – and an amount per pupil. There are different rates for primary (£11.25), secondary (£16.88), post-16 (£22.50) and special/PRU (£33.75). As with any grant funding it is subject to change or abolition.

Condition improvement fund (CIF)

▷ Academy trusts must bid to the ESFA for CIF funding. Priority is given to academies in which the buildings are in poor condition and will require significant investment to improve. It also provides more limited funding to expand the facilities at academies – these must be rated good or outstanding.

▷ Only single academy trusts and small MATs (fewer than five schools and 3,000 pupils) can bid for funding through the CIF. Larger MATs are provided with capital funding through the School Condition Allocation (see below).

▷ The call for bids usually goes out in autumn and closes at the end of December. If successful, academy trusts are required to meet the conditions of grant funding and report on their spending.

School Condition Allocation (SCA)

▷ MATs with more than five schools and 3,000 pupils receive SCA funding as well as devolved formula capital funding. The SCA is allocated via a complex formula. It takes into account pupil numbers, but also the condition of the buildings. It is for the trustee board to determine how to spend the SCA across their estate.

Checklist

▷ Schedule regular reports to trustees giving a clear picture of the condition of the premises and buildings.

▷ Details of the capital grant(s) the academy trust received.
▷ Proposed bids for CIF.

▷ Is there a plan for spending the devolved formula capital?

▷ Is there a plan for spending the SCA based on an objective assessment of the trust's school estate?

Procedure

▷ Trustees should receive regular reports about the state of the premises/buildings it is responsible for.

▷ There should be clear schedule for premises improvement works.

▷ Proposal to submit a bid for CIF funding should be submitted and approved by trustees.

Notes

▷ There is limited capital funding available and trustees need to be sure that any funding received is being used in the most effective way possible.

More information

▷ DfE Capital funding websites:

▷ www.gov.uk/government/publications/capital-allocations
▷ www.gov.uk/search?q=condition+improvement+fund
▷ www.gov.uk/guidance/capital-funding-for-multi-academy-trusts-mats

▷ DfE Estates Management Guidance: www.gov.uk/guidance/good-estate-management-for-schools

▷ *Academy Governance Handbook*, Chapter 11.

Chair of trustees – appointment

Introduction

All academy trusts are required by their articles of association to appoint a chair of trustees. The Articles will stipulate who has the power to appoint the chair; in most academy trusts this will be via a vote of the trustees, but in trusts where there is a principal sponsor the position of chair may be in the gift of the principal sponsor.

The current model articles stipulate that the chair will be elected annually by the trustees.

The academy trust must notify the ESFA within 14 days where a new chair is appointed. The notification must be through the DfE's GIAS website.

The Education (Independent School Standards) Regulations 2014 require that chairs of academy trusts have an enhanced Disclosure and Barring service (DBS) check which has been counter-signed by the Secretary of State for Education.

It is good practice for the academy trust to approve a written role description for the chair and for this to be reviewed and amended from time to time.

The AFH 2018 states that 'The chair of trustees is responsible for ensuring the effective functioning of the board and setting professional standards of governance'.

Where it is for the trustees to appoint a chair, it is also good practice to adopt a formal procedure for doing this. Good practice is for nominations for chair to be submitted in advance of the meeting at which time the vote will take place and for the decision to be made by secret ballot.

The DfE provides funding for a development course for chairs or prospective chairs of boards. This can be accessed through five approved providers.

Checklist

▷ Check the articles for who has the power to appoint the chair.

▶ Check if the trustees have adopted rules and procedures for the appointment of the chair.

▶ Review the role description and update as appropriate.

▶ Notify the ESFA within 14 days if a new chair is appointed.

▶ Arrange for a DBS check to be counter-signed by the Secretary of State.

▶ Consider what development needs the new chair might have.

Procedure

▶ Follow all the appropriate procedures to make the appointment – both those set out in the articles and any additional procedures adopted by the trustees.

▶ Ensure decision is recorded in the minutes of the trustees' meeting.

▶ Notify the ESFA of the appointment.

▶ Ensure appropriate DBS checks are put in train.

▶ Update the trust's website with the name of the chair.

Filing requirements

▶ The ESFA must be notified of the change via the DfE (GIAS) website within 14 days.

▶ The trust's website must be updated with the new information.

Notes

▶ The academy trust should have a succession plan in place for the position of the chair – even if the chair has only just taken up office. If the academy trust has set limits on how long a chair can serve, then it is vital that succession planning is put in place to fit with that. If the articles of association do not set a limit it would be good governance practice for the trustees to set their own rules to introduce a limit.

▶ Where a limit is in place everyone is clear about how long the chair will serve. This enables succession planning to be timetabled, but also prevents the awkwardness of having to ask an incumbent not to stand again – or facing an unexpected election.

▶ At the very least the trustees should ascertain whether there is a current member of the board who would be willing and have the skills to take the chair if the current incumbent stepped down.

▶ The chair has a role to play in succession planning. Ideally, the chair should indicate at least a year before they step down that they intend to do so, in order for the succession plan to be in place.

▶ The Inspiring Governance service has a Future Chairs project which is delivered by the NGA – there is a bespoke service for boards in certain areas of the country who have no one on their board at present who is interested in stepping up once the current chair steps down but do want to plan ahead. Boards in the non-priority areas can also use the Inspiring Governance recruitment service to look for individuals who have indicated that they have previous experience of chairing and would be wiling to do so again.

More information

▶ Academy Governance Checklists:

▷ Get information about schools (GIAS);
▷ Chair of trustees – role and responsibilities.

▶ DfE – Guidance on DBS checks for chairs of academy trusts: www.gov.uk/guidance/enhanced-dbs-disclosure-checks-for-chairs-of-academy-trusts

▶ DfE funded governance leadership development programmes: www.gov.uk/guidance/school-governors-professional-development#governance-leadership-development-programme

▶ NGA Preparing your board for the future: A guide to succession planning: www.nga.org.uk/Guidance/Workings-Of-The-Governing-Body/Chairs-of-Governors/Preparing-your-board-for-the-future.aspx

▶ Inspiring Governance future chairs project: www.nga.org.uk/Be-a-Governor/Future-Chairs-Recruitment-Service.aspx

▶ *Academy Governance Handbook*, Chapter 4.

Chair of trustees – cessation of office

Introduction

It is considered best practice for there to be regular turnover among trustees and this is true for the chair of the board.

Unlike many charities, most academy trust articles do not restrict the length of time an individual can serve as a trustee or chair. It is open to trustees to set their own limits on how long an individual can serve as chair. The National Governance Association recommends that chairs should normally expect to stand down after six years in the position.

Checklist

▶ Chairs may cease to hold office for a variety of reasons:

▷ voluntary resignation as chair – the articles of associations for most academy trusts do not require a chair to also step down as a trustee when they cease office as chair. However, it is considered by many good practice for the chair to step down from the board at the point they cease to be chair – it is not always helpful for the new chair to have the old chair looking over their shoulder. The model articles allow for a chair to resign at any point;

▷ cessation of office as a trustee – the model articles require that the chair is a trustee;

▷ non reappointment as chair – the model articles require that the chair stands for reappointment each school year;

▷ they take up employment with the academy trust – no one employed by an academy trust can serve as chair;

▷ they are removed from office in accordance with the articles of association; or

▷ they are disqualified for any reason as a charity trustee or company director.

Procedure

Resignation

▶ It is best practice to obtain a written letter of resignation.

▶ Ensure the resignation is noted in the minutes of the next relevant meeting. The minutes should also record if the trustee remains a trustee after resigning as chair.

▶ The ESFA will need to be notified via GIAS, within 14 days.

▶ If the chair has also resigned as a trustee/director then Companies House will need to be informed.

▶ The relevant registers will also need to be amended if the chair has also resigned as a trustee/director.

▶ Update the trust's website and any other relevant material.

▶ The model articles of association stipulate that the vice chair will act as chair if there is a vacancy for chair.

Removal from office

▶ It is generally better to try to persuade the chair to resign than to use formal removal procedures. This should be very much a last resort and would generally indicate that there are serious issues within the trust.

Procedure

▶ The resolution to remove the chair must be a stated item of business on the agenda of a trustees' meeting.

▶ Good practice would be to provide the chair with detailed reasons for the proposal in advance of the meeting.

▶ Ensure the meeting is quorate.

▶ Trustee proposing the removal should state their reasons.

▶ Chair must be given the opportunity to respond.

▶ Proposal should be put to a vote – a simple majority is required.

▶ The resolution must be put to a second meeting not less than 14 days after the first meeting. The removal of the chair must be a stated item of business.

▶ Proposal must be put to a second vote. If confirmed the chair is removed.

▶ Minutes should record the removal.

▶ The ESFA should be notified via GIAS.

Other cessations of office

▶ Most of the steps set out under resignation procedure will apply.

Notes

▶ The academy trust should have a succession plan in place for the position of the chair – even if the chair has only just taken up office. At the very least the trustees should ascertain whether there is a current member of the board who would be willing and have the skills to take the chair if the current incumbent stepped down.

More information

▶ Academies Governance Checklists: Chair of trustees – role and responsibilities.

▶ AFH 2018: www.gov.uk/government/publications/academies-financial-handbook

▶ NGA Preparing your board for the future: A guide to succession planning: www.nga.org.uk/Guidance/Workings-Of-The-Governing-Body/Chairs-of-Governors/Preparing-your-board-for-the-future.aspx

Chair of trustees – role and responsibilities

Introduction

Every board needs a chair to oversee the running of the board and chair meetings – it is a requirement of an academy trust's articles that there is a chair of the board.

It is good practice for the board to approve a written role description for the chair and for this to be reviewed and updated periodically. The role description should be consistent with the academy trust's articles of association.

Checklist

Role

'The chair of trustees is responsible for ensuring the effective functioning of the board and setting professional standards of governance.' (AFH 2018)

Responsibilities – general

The chair's principal responsibilities are to:

▷ provide leadership to the trustee board and ensure that trustees fulfil their functions for the proper governance of the academy trust;

▷ ensure the governing board sets a clear vision and strategy for academy trust;

▷ ensure the board has the required skills to fulfil its responsibilities;

▷ build a professional relationship with the senior executive leader which allows for honest conversations, acting as a sounding board and ensuring there are no surprises at meetings;

▷ ensure the board's business is focused on the key strategic priorities;

▷ with the clerk/governance professional and the senior executive leader to plan for the board meetings, ensuring that agendas focus on the board's key responsibilities and strategic priorities;

- ensure that decisions taken at the meetings of the governing body are implemented;

- take the lead in encouraging board self-evaluation and review and that of individual trustees;

- where required, represent the trustee board in its dealings with external partners and be an advocate for the trust and take the lead in representing the trustee board at relevant external meetings with agencies such as the DfE, ESFA and Ofsted; and

- chair meetings effectively and promote an open culture that allows all trustees to contribute to discussion and ensure that the trustees make well-thought-through decisions.

Additional responsibilities

- In some trusts the chair may also be responsible for chairing meetings of members – the articles of association will state whether this is the case.

Filing requirements

- The ESFA need to be notified via GIAS of the name of the chair.

- The chair's name must be published on the trust's website.

- The chair should be identified in the trustees' annual report.

More information

- Academy Governance Checklists:
  - Get information about schools (GIAS);
  - Chair of trustees – appointment;
  - Chair of trustees – cessation of office.

- DfE – Guidance on DBS checks for chairs of academy trusts: www.gov.uk/guidance/enhanced-dbs-disclosure-checks-for-chairs-of-academy-trusts

- DfE funded governance leadership development programmes: www.gov.uk/guidance/school-governors-professional-development#governance-leadership-development-programme

- NGA Preparing your board for the future: A guide to succession planning: www.nga.org.uk/Guidance/Workings-Of-The-Governing-Body/Chairs-of-Governors/Preparing-your-board-for-the-future.aspx

- Inspiring Governance future chairs project: www.nga.org.uk/Be-a-Governor/Future-Chairs-Recruitment-Service.aspx

Charitable status

Introduction

Being a charity carries specific legal responsibilities in the way its funds and assets are managed. This is true whether the organisation is a registered charity, or an exempt charity, such as academy trusts.

Exempt charities are subject to charity law and must have regard to guidance issued by the Charity Commission for England and Wales. Charity status confers certain duties and obligations on those running the organisation:

▶ To be a charity in England or Wales, the organisation must be set up with purposes which are exclusively charitable for the public benefit.

▶ The Charities Act 2011 describes a charitable purpose as one which falls within 13 definitions of purposes. All academy trusts have as one of their objects, the advancement of education – some trusts have additional objects.

Checklist

▶ The academy trust must pursue its own charitable purpose (as set out in the articles of association) and must do so for the public benefit.

▶ The funds and assets must be protected and used correctly, towards the charitable purposes of the academy trust an in accordance with charity law restrictions and requirements.

▶ No significant private or commercial benefits must arise from the academy trust's activities (any such benefits must be only those that are necessary and incidental to the pursuit of charitable objects).

▶ The academy trust is regulated by charity law and overseen by the relevant charity regulator (i.e. the DfE/ESFA).

▶ The academy trust is publicly accountable and must provide detailed annual accounts and an annual trustees' report.

▶ The members have no commercial interest – they do not 'own' the charity in the way that the members of a commercial company do.

▶ The trustees are stewards and custodians with legal duties.

More information

▶ Academy Governance Checklists:

  ▷ Charity Commission for England and Wales;
  ▷ Department for Education (DfE);
  ▷ Education and Skills Funding Agency;
  ▷ Exempt charity status.

▶ *Academy Governance Handbook*, Chapter 2.

Charity Commission for England and Wales

Introduction

The Charity Commission for England is the charity regulator for all registered charities in England.

Charity Commission – legal basis

The legal basis for the Charity Commission is set out in the Charities Act 2011.

The commission is a corporate body with statutory objectives functions and duties.

The Commission is independent of government and outside the direction and control of Ministers. It is accountable to Parliament through the Home Secretary and is ultimately answerable to the Courts.

Charity Commission – statutory objectives

These are to:

- increase public trust and confidence in charities ('the public confidence objective');
- promote awareness and understanding of the operation of the public benefit requirement ('the public benefit objective');
- promote compliance by charity trustees with their legal obligations in exercising control and management of the administration of their charities ('the compliance objective');
- promote the effective use of charitable resources ('the charitable resources objective'); and
- enhance the accountability of charities to donors, beneficiaries and the general public ('the accountability objective').

Charity Commission – statement of mission, regulatory approach and values

The Charity Commission set out in its Statement of mission, regulatory approach and values (2017) how it considers it can best fulfil its statutory objectives by concentrating on the following:

▶ promoting compliance by charity trustees with their legal obligations;

▶ enhancing transparency and the rigour with which it holds charities accountable;

▶ promoting the effective use of charitable resources by raising awareness, supporting trustees and enabling them to comply with their duties; and

▶ ensuring that only bodies that properly qualify as charities under the law are registered.

Role in relation to academy trusts

▶ Academy trusts are exempt charities which means they do not need to register with the Charity Commission and are regulated by a principal regulator, the Secretary of State for Education, whose powers are exercised by the Department for Education and its executive agency, the ESFA.

▶ The Charity Commission retains an interest in compliance and in addressing non-compliance with legal or regulatory requirements or misconduct or mismanagement in the administration of any charity, including academy trusts. It retains some powers over exempt charities, and consequently Academy Trusts. In most cases its powers will only be exercised after consultation with the DfE as principal regulator. It may also investigate academy trusts, but only if invited to do so by the principal regulator.

▶ Principal regulators have a duty under the Charities Act to do all they reasonably can to promote compliance by the trustees of the charities for which they are responsible with their legal obligations in exercising control and management of the administration of their charity.

Charity Commission and DfE – Memorandum of Understanding (MoU)

▶ The DfE and the Charity Commission have signed an MoU. The MoU sets out how the Charity Commission for England and Wales and the DfE, including its executive agency – the ESFA – propose to work together and communicate effectively, in relation to their regulatory responsibilities.

▶ It sets out the powers of the Charity Commission and DfE in relation to academy trusts.

More information

▶ Charity Commission and DfE – Memorandum of Understanding: www.gov.uk/government/publications/memorandum-of-understanding-charity-commission-and-the-department-for-education

▶ DfE – AFH 2018 (para 1.2.9).

▶ ICSA Charity Checklists – Charity regulators.

▶ *Academy Governance Handbook*, Chapter 2.

Charity Governance Code

Introduction

The Charity Governance Code is a sector-developed code. It is designed as a tool to support continuous improvement of the board. The code is organised around seven principles:

- organisational purpose;
- leadership;
- integrity;
- decision making, risk and control;
- board effectiveness;
- diversity; and
- openness and accountability.

For each principle there is a rationale (the reason why it is important), key outcomes (what you would expect to see if the principle were adopted) and recommended practice (what actions might be taken to implement the principles).

While the code has no statutory power, it is closely aligned to the Nolan principles and is endorsed by the Charity Commission.

The provisions in the Charity Governance Code are considered best practice and academy trusts would not go far wrong in following and adopting its recommended practices.

Procedure

- Standards of good governance and best practice should be considered and followed as far as practicable in the circumstances.

Filing requirements

None.

More information

▶ Charity Governance Code: www.charitygovernancecode.org/en/front-page

▶ Academy Governance Checklists:

    ▷ Good governance – principles of;
    ▷ UK Corporate Governance Code.

▶ *Academy Governance Handbook*, Chapter 1.

Chief executive officer

Introduction

The chief executive officer (CEO) is generally the most senior member of staff of an organisation and is responsible for day-to-day operations.

The AFH 2018 requires that the trustees appoint a senior executive leader who will be responsible for the day-to-day management of the trust. While there are a range of titles given to the senior executive leader across all academy trusts, in MATs they are generally known as the chief executive officer.

The model articles of association stipulate that the trustees shall appoint the chief executive and may delegate such powers and functions as they consider are required by them for the internal organisation, management and control of the organisation, including the implementation of all policies approved by the trustees and for the direction of the teaching and curriculum at the academies in the trust.

The trustee board has strategic responsibility for the organisation and should, therefore, ensure that it has delegated all powers and function to the CEO for the effective operational running to the academy trust.

The AFH 2018 requires that trustees appoint an accounting officer and the expectation is that this will be the CEO.

Appointment

▷ The role of CEO is different to that of headteacher/principal of a SAT – it requires different skills. Many MATs have grown from a single original school and there has been a temptation to appoint the original headteacher as the CEO. Not all excellent headteachers make good CEOs. Before making any appointments, trustees need to have developed a clear role description and person specification, and assess candidates against that role descriptor.

CEO as trustee

▷ In the current model articles the CEO does not have an automatic right to be a trustee – although if they agree to act, the members can appoint them. Earlier versions of the articles did give the CEO a right to be a trustee.

▶ The NGA does not think it is good practice for the CEO to be a trustee, considering that the dual role of 'presenting plans, giving advice and providing information' to the board creates an inherent conflict of interest if they are at the same time a member of that board.

▶ It is important that the CEO attends trustee meetings to provide information and contribute to discussion.

Checklist

▶ Appoint the senior executive leader in line with the articles of association and good recruitment practice.

▶ Ensure the necessary safeguarding checks are carried out.

▶ Ensure the necessary powers and functions are delegated to the CEO to enable effective day-to-day operation of the trust and that this is recorded in writing in the SoD.

▶ Appoint the accounting officer in writing.

Procedure

▶ Appoint the CEO in line with trust recruitment policies.

▶ Provide delegated authority to run the trust to the CEO.

▶ Record delegated authorities in the SoD.

▶ Notify the ESFA of the appointment via the DfE's GIAS website.

Filing requirements

▶ The ESFA must be informed of the CEO's appointment via the DfE's GIAS website.

▶ The academy trust's website should record the name of the CEO.

More information

▶ Trust's articles of association.

▶ AFH 2018.

▶ DfE *Governance Handbook*.

▶ Academy Governance Checklists:

▷ Accounting officer;
▷ Executive headteacher;
▷ Principal;
▷ Senior executive leader.

▶ *Academy Governance Handbook*, Chapter 4.

Chief financial officer

Introduction

The Chief Financial Officer (CFO) is the person in the trust who has day-to-day responsibility for the financial management of the trust. They may be called chief operating officer, finance director or business manager; whatever their title they will be the person who has responsibility for the trust's detailed financial procedures.

The role has two aspects, technical and leadership: technical in that this person is responsible for ensuring proper financial processes that meet legal requirements are in place and leadership in ensuring these are followed and implemented properly.

The AFH requires that the trustees appoint a CFO. The trustees should ensure that the CFO has the appropriate level of skill and experience for the role – it is open to trustees to determine the precise level and nature of qualifications required for the role. This will vary depending on the size and complexity of the trust.

Checklist

▷ Ensure an appropriately skilled CFO has been appointed in line with trust recruitment policies.
▷ Notify the ESFA of the appointment within 14 days via the governance section of the DfE's GIAS website.

Procedure

▷ Appoint a CFO in line with trust recruitment policies.

Filing requirements

▷ Notify the ESFA using the governance section of the DfE GIAS website.

More information

▷ AFH 2018.
▷ Academy Governance Checklists: Financial scheme of delegation.
▷ DfE GIAS.
▷ *Academy Governance Handbook*, Chapter 12.

Clerk to the board

Introduction

It is generally recognised that all boards require high-quality support to enable them to function effectively. In academy trusts this is provided by the clerk who may also act as secretary and in MATs may be called a governance professional.

The DfE's Clerking Competency Framework says that there are three key things a clerk should provide the board with:

▷ administrative and organisational support;

▷ guidance to ensure that the board works in compliance with the appropriate legal and regulatory framework, and understands the potential consequences for non-compliance; and

▷ advice on procedural matters relating to the operation of the board.

The Framework recognises that different types of school organisations will require different levels of support. In a MAT the 'governance support' is now often provided by a governance professional, who oversees clerking at academy level.

All academy trust articles of association require that the trustee board appoints a clerk to the board (although in some articles the clerk will be styled as secretary). The clerk cannot be the senior executive leader or a trustee.

As private companies, academy trusts are not required to appoint a company secretary, but where they do, they can choose to give the clerk a dual role or appoint another individual to that role.

Checklist

Trustees' role

▷ Trustees to appoint a clerk.

▷ Where a clerk cannot attend a meeting, to appoint an individual from among their number to minute that meeting.

Clerk's role

▶ Organise board/committee meetings.

▶ Agree meeting agendas with the chair and senior executive leader.

▶ Ensure trustee board and committee meetings are properly constituted, quorate.

▶ Advise the chair and agree with them an annual schedule of business for the board.

▶ Ensure that the board and committee agendas are co-ordinated.

▶ Advise the board on compliance matters and ensure correct procedures are followed.

▶ Provide independent and impartial advice to the board on governance matters.

▶ Draft accurate and timely minutes of board and committee meetings.

▶ Facilitate the induction, professional development and evaluation of trustees including skills audits to ensure appropriate composition of the board.

Procedure

▶ Trustees to organise the appointment of the clerk.

Notes

▶ The importance of a professional clerk cannot be over-stated. It ensures that the board functions effectively and has access to high-quality advice on its governance functions.

▶ 'I want to be very clear that governance professionals are the cornerstone of effective governance: they are vital. The role of governance professionals is not only about good and effective organisation and administration, but also, and more importantly, about helping the board understand its role, functions and legal duties.' (Lord Agnew, Parliamentary under Secretary of State for the School System, February 2019)

▶ In recruiting a clerk trustees should follow proper recruitment procedures, and ensure that they develop a role description and person specification. Too often in the school sector the length of time needed to undertake clerking duties is underestimated so trustees should ensure that they include in the contract enough time for the duties to be completed.

▶ The DfE has funded development programmes for clerks which can be accessed via five providers approved by the DfE. The NGA's development programme for clerks is accredited by ICSA.

More information

▶ Academy Governance Checklists:

   ▷ Company secretary;
   ▷ Governance professional.

▶ DfE:

   ▷ Clerking Competency Framework: www.gov.uk/government/publications/governance-handbook
   ▷ Governance Handbook: www.gov.uk/government/publications/governance-handbook
   ▷ Academy Trust Articles of association
   ▷ NGA's Leading Governance – Clerking Development Programme: www.nga.org.uk/LeadingGovernance/Clerks.aspx

▶ *Academy Governance Handbook*, Chapter 5.

Clerking Competency Framework (DfE)

Introduction

The Clerking Competency Framework is non-statutory guidance from the DfE which sets out the competencies it thinks are required to deliver professional clerking across all types of state-funded schools. The framework recognises that different types of setting will have different clerking needs.

The Framework is structured around four competencies:

▷ Understanding governance – the board's duties, responsibilities, governance legislation and procedures in order that the clerk can contribute to the effectiveness of the board. Such knowledge will lead to better-quality advice on legal and procedural matters related to governance; make for more accurate recording of discussions and decisions; and enable more efficient use of the board's time.

▷ Administration – professional clerking ensures that the processes and procedures of governance are administered efficiently. Taking care of the basics enables the chair and the board to make more effective use of their time and focus on strategic matters.

▷ Advice and guidance – access to timely and accurate advice and guidance, or signposting to expert advice where appropriate, contributes to better and more efficient decision-making and helps the board to manage the risk of non-compliance with legal and regulatory frameworks.

▷ People and relationships – professional clerking builds and maintains professional working relationships with the board, which is the foundation for providing impartial advice and support. Good relationships are also essential to establishing open communication and ensuring smooth information flow between the board, the executive leaders and, where required, staff, parents and the local community.

Notes

▷ The Framework can be used for both recruitment and developmental purposes.

▶ The DfE clerking development programmes are structured around the Clerking Competency Framework.

More information

▶ Academy Governance Checklists:

▷ Clerk to the board;
▷ Company secretary;
▷ Governance professional.

▶ DfE:

▷ Clerking Competency Framework: www.gov.uk/government/publications/governance-handbook
▷ Governance Handbook: www.gov.uk/government/publications/governance-handbook

▶ NGA Clerking Development Programme, ICSA accredited: www.nga.org.uk/LeadingGovernance/Clerks.aspx

▶ *Academy Governance Handbook*, Chapter 5.

Code of Conduct

Introduction

It is good practice for trustee boards to adopt a code of conduct.

A code of conduct will set out general standards of behaviour in relation to how trustees deal both with each other and employees.

The code of conduct should be included as part of the recruitment pack for new trustees, so they are clear about what is expected of them. The code of conduct should be rooted in the Nolan principles of public life.

More recently the Commission for Ethical Leadership in Education has published its Ethical Leadership in Education Framework and it is well worth trustees and senior leaders considering the framework and deciding whether to adopt its principles. The framework takes the Nolan principles as its starting point and applies them specifically to a school setting.

Checklist

- Adopt a trustee board code of conduct.
- Use the code of conduct as part of the information pack for prospective trustees.
- Consider adopting the Framework for Ethical Leadership in Education.

Procedure

- Adoption of the code of conduct should be an item on the agenda at the first trustees' meeting of the year.
- Trustees can be requested to sign the document, but if the trustee board formally adopts it then all trustees will be bound by it.

More information

- Academy Governance Checklists: Nolan principles and the framework for ethical leadership in education.
- *Academy Governance Handbook*, Chapter 9.

Collective worship

Introduction

All academy trusts are required through their funding agreements (master or supplementaries) to ensure that all pupils in all their academies are delivered a daily act of collective worship.

DfE Circular 1/94 sets out the requirements for collective worship and religious education. It states:

'Collective worship in schools should aim to provide the opportunity for pupils to worship God, to consider spiritual and moral issues and to explore their own beliefs; to encourage participation and response, whether through active involvement in the presentation of worship or through listening to and joining in the worship offered; and to develop community spirit, promote a common ethos and shared values, and reinforce positive attitudes.'

For all schools without a religious character the default position is that the daily act of collective worship should be 'wholly or mainly or a broadly Christian character'. Where a majority of the pupils in the school are from non-Christian backgrounds then it is possible to seek a determination to carry out the daily act of worship in another religious faith.

Where any academy is designated as having a religious character and was a former foundation or voluntary aided school then the daily act of collective worship will be delivered according 'to the tenets and practices of the academy's specified religion or religious denomination'.

Companies House

Introduction

Companies House is the official public registry of companies in the UK. It is an Executive Agency of the Department for Business, Innovation and Skills.

The legislation governing company registration is set out in the CA2006.

Companies (including academy trusts) are required to file a range of documents and information with Companies House, some on an annual basis (e.g. confirmation statement and annual return and accounts) and some as information changes (e.g. director appointments and terminations).

The most popular and straightforward way and cheapest way to file information is via the electronic web filing system. This requires a user to register via the Companies House website. The user will then be provided with a unique user passcode. You can only file information for a company if you are a registered user. In addition, any company that wants to file data electronically must first obtain an authentication code, which will be posted to the registered office address.

The main functions of Companies House are to:

▷ incorporate and dissolve companies;

▷ examine and store company information delivered under the CA2006 and related legislation; and

▷ make this information available to the public.

Checklist

▷ Ensure that all relevant returns are submitted to Companies House.

▷ Confirmation statement must be filed every 12 months.

▷ Annual return and accounts must be filed with Companies House within nine months of the end of academy trusts' financial year (i.e. by 31 May).

▷ Sign up for company web filing.

Notes

▶ Companies House published a range of guidance to assist companies on complying with their public filing and reporting requirements.

▶ Companies registered for electronic filing will receive updates to any change of practice or requirements from Companies House as well as reminders of the need to file certain documents (e.g. confirmation statement).

More information

▶ Academy Governance Checklists:

  ▷ Accounts – academies consolidated annual report and accounts;
  ▷ Confirmation statement;
  ▷ Register of persons with significant control.

▶ Companies House: www.gov.uk/government/organisations/companies-house

▶ *Academy Governance Handbook*, Chapter 5.

Company secretary

Introduction

Company secretary is a formal designated role and the holder of this office is classed as an officer of the company and recorded at Companies House as such.

Private companies (such as academy trusts) need only appoint a designated company secretary if this requirement is stipulated in their articles of association. The model articles for academy trusts do not contain this provision, but trusts may appoint a company secretary if they choose.

There is no legal definition of the role of company secretary but in most corporate organisations this is a relatively senior role with considerable responsibilities for governance arrangements and providing detailed advice.

This is a relatively new role to the state-funded school sector. State-funded schools have 'clerks to the governing board', but until recently the importance of a 'professional' clerk has been under-appreciated; consequently the role has not had the level of seniority or remuneration that one would find in many company secretarial roles.

Where a trust is choosing to designate an individual as company secretary then this must be covered in their terms and conditions of employment and the specific responsibilities clearly stated. There is a significant difference between designating someone as company secretary whose only responsibilities relate to filing returns to Companies House, compared to someone who is the senior governance professional in the organisation and expected to provide advice and guidance to the board on their roles and responsibilities.

Regardless of whether the academy trust chooses to formally designate someone as company secretary, it is required to file documents with Companies House and consequently someone needs to have this responsibility.

It is for the trustees to determine whether to appoint a company secretary and if so, who that should be.

Checklist

▶ For trustees:

   ▷ consider whether to appoint a company secretary;
   ▷ where appointing, ensure there is a clear role description.

The company secretary role in its widest sense includes the following:

For the trustee board

▶ Organise board/committee meetings.

▶ Agree meeting agendas with the chair and senior executive leader.

▶ Ensure trustee board and committee meetings are properly constituted, quorate.

▶ Advise the chair and agree with them an annual schedule of business for the board.

▶ Ensure that the board and committee agendas are co-ordinated.

▶ Advise the board on compliance matters and ensure correct procedures are followed.

▶ Provide independent and impartial advice to the board on governance matters.

▶ Ensure the trustees are acting in accordance with the articles of association, Companies Act, Charity law and DfE and ESFA guidance.

▶ Draft accurate and timely minutes of board and committee meetings.

▶ Facilitate the induction, professional development and evaluation of trustees including skills audits to ensure appropriate composition of the board.

Register and returns

▶ Maintain statutory registers (members, directors and secretary).

▶ Ensure the company meets the regular filing requirements of Companies House and report changes relating to the company, including:

   ▷ approved amendments to the articles of association;
   ▷ notice of appointment, resignation and removal of directors and the secretary;
   ▷ notices of removal or resignation of the auditors;
   ▷ change of registered office;
   ▷ company resolutions;
   ▷ confirmation statement;
   ▷ report and accounts (company auditors will often undertake to file these).

For the company/members

▶ Organise general meetings as required by the articles of association.

▶ Prepare and issue notices of meetings and proxy forms.

▶ Support the trustee board and prepare briefing notes as necessary.

▶ Ensure correct procedures are followed, especially in relation to voting.

Reports and accounts

▶ Co-ordinate the preparation, publication and distribution of the company's annual report and accounts.

▶ Assist the trustees with the narrative sections of the annual report, particularly relating to the work of the trustees and their committees.

Notes

▶ The company secretary is regarded as an 'officer' of the trust company. This means that they can sign the majority of forms for filing at Companies House (though in practice this is largely now done online). They can also be a signatory to any documents that need the signatures of two officers of the trust company. This does also mean that the company secretary can find themselves potentially liable as an 'officer in default' with respect to breaches of the Companies Act provisions.

More information

▶ Academy Governance Checklists:

  ▷ Clerk to the board;
  ▷ Governance professional.

▶ *Academy Governance Handbook*, Chapter 5.

Competency Framework for Governance (DfE)

Introduction

The Competency Framework for Governance was published by the DfE in 2017 and aims to set out the knowledge, skills and behaviours needed for effective governance in all types of state-funded schools.

Six features of effective governance

The document is structured around the DfE's six features of effective governance. These are identified as:

- strategic leadership;

- accountability;

- people;

- structures;

- compliance; and

- evaluation.

Sixteen competencies are identified across the six features and for each competency the document sets out the skills and knowledge needed to govern effectively. It splits this down into things which:

- the whole board need to know and do;

- the chair needs to know and do; or

- someone on the board needs to know and do.

Key attributes

Underpinning the competencies are the key principles and attributes that all those governing will need. These are to be: committed, confident, curious, challenging, collaborative, critical and creative.

The framework can be used to:

- inform a skills audit of the board;

- help develop a role descriptor for a trustee/chair;

▷ inform conversations with individual trustees about their contributions over the year; and

▷ identify areas for board development.

Notes

▷ The framework needs to be considered in the context of the organisation. Not all competencies will be applicable to all settings. For example, those sitting on academy committees in MATs, will not be responsible for the same range of governance functions that those on MAT trustee boards will.

▷ As a result of trying to cover the range of governance models which now occur in state-funded schools, the document is a somewhat unwieldy 27 pages.

▷ The document should be used to put together a skills audit for the board, rather than as checklist. Alternatively use a skills audit (such as the NGAs), which has already been adapted for different settings using the Competency Framework.

More information

▷ Academy Governance Checklists: Board skills audit and register.

▷ DfE:

 ▷ Competency Framework for Governance: www.gov.uk/government/publications/governance-handbook
 ▷ *Governance Handbook*: www.gov.uk/government/publications/governance-handbook

▷ NGA Skills Audit: www.nga.org.uk/Guidance/Workings-Of-The-Governing-Body/Governance-Tools/Skills-Audit.aspx

▷ *Academy Governance Handbook*, Chapter 2.

Complaints procedures

Introduction

In accordance with the Education (Independent School Standards) Regulations 2014 all academy trusts are required to adopt complaints procedures for dealing with complaints from parents of pupils.

The Regulations set out what should be included in the procedure.

Checklist

The academy trust must adopt a complaints procedure which meets the requirement of the Regulations.

The Regulations stipulate that the complaints procedure must:

▶ be in writing;

▶ be made available to parents of pupils;

▶ set out clear timescales for the management of a complaint;

▶ allow for a complaint to be made and considered initially on an informal basis;

▶ where the parent is not satisfied with the response establish a formal procedure for the complaint to be made in writing;

▶ where the parent is still not satisfied, make provision for a hearing before a panel appointed by or on behalf of the proprietor and consisting of at least three people who were not directly involved in the matters detailed in the complaint;

▶ ensure that where there is a panel hearing of a complaint, one panel member is independent of the management and running of the school;

▶ allow for a parent to attend and be accompanied at a panel hearing if they wish;

▶ provide for the panel to make findings and recommendations and stipulate that a copy of those findings and recommendations is:

> provided to the complainant and, where relevant, the person complained about; and
> available for inspection on the school premises by the proprietor and the headteacher;

▶ provide for a written record to be kept of all complaints that are made, and action taken by the school as a result of those complaints (regardless of whether they are upheld); and

▶ provide that correspondence, statements and records relating to individual complaints are to be kept confidential except where the Secretary of State or a body conducting an inspection under section 109 of the 2008 Act requests access to them.

Procedure

▶ Adopt a complaints procedure which meets the requirement of the Education (Independent Schools Standards) Regulations 2014.

Notes

▶ All organisations at some point, however well run, will be the subject of a complaint. How they deal with that complaint can be as important as the outcome.

More information

▶ ESFA guidance on setting up and academy complaints procedure: www.gov.uk/government/publications/setting-up-an-academies-complaints-procedure

▶ *Academy Governance Handbook*, Chapter 7.

Confederation of School Trusts

Introduction

The Confederation of School Trusts (CST), formerly (FASNA), is a charitable company and national membership organisation for school trusts.

The CST seeks to speaks for and provide support to those running school trusts, both executives and trustees.

The CST runs conferences, provides information and guidance and is one of the organisations licensed to provide DfE development programmes for those governing and clerks.

More information

▶ https://cstuk.org.uk

Confirmation statement

Introduction

Every company must file a confirmation statement annually at Companies House (using form CS01). The statement confirms that all the information that the company is required to have delivered to Companies House has been delivered or is being delivered at the same time as the confirmation statement.

The statement must be made either:

▶ not more than 12 months after the previous conformation statement; or

▶ 12 months after incorporation.

It must be filed in writing within 14 days of the confirmation date, together with a fee, which is currently £13 (electronic) or £40 (hard copy).

Checklist

▶ Ensure that the person responsible for submitting the confirmation statement has a reminder of when it is done.

▶ Check if the details held at Companies House are up to date and either confirm or complete the confirmation statement along with any additional forms required to update the public record.

The following information will need to be reviewed and confirmed:

▶ the name of the trust;

▶ the registered number;

▶ the date to which the confirmation statement is made up;

▶ the standard industrial classification (SIC) code (see below);

▶ the principal business activities of the company;

▶ the type of company (e.g. private);

▶ the registered office address;

▶ the address (single alternate inspection location – SAIL) where the company keeps certain company records if not at the registered office, and the records held there;

- company secretary (corporate or individual), where applicable;

- the company's trustees (corporate or individual); and

- people with significant control (PSCs).

Procedures

- First review begins on the date of incorporation and ends 12 months later. Subsequent review periods are 12 months starting from the day after the previous confirmation statement.

- A confirmation statement is required even where there have been no changes.

- For all companies details of any relevant changes should be made during the year as they happen or otherwise using appropriate forms at the same time as the statements.

Filing requirements

- Form CS01.

- Filing fee: £13 electronically or £40 hard copy.

Notes

- The details supplied on the confirmation statement are a snapshot of the information accurate at a particular date known as the 'made-up date'. A trust may submit confirmation statements as often as it wishes provided it files at least one every 12 months.

- Companies House allows for web filing and if signed up to web filing then electronic reminders will be sent off when the confirmation statement is due.

- The confirmation statement includes a 'standard industrial classification' (SIC) code of five digits which identifies the company's business. A trust could have more than one SIC code where it operates across phases. In the case of academies, the relevant codes will usually be:

  ▷ 85100 Pre-primary education;
  ▷ 85200 Primary education;
  ▷ 85310 General secondary education;
  ▷ 85320 Technical and vocational secondary education.

- The trustees and secretary (where applicable) are responsible for filing the confirmation statement on time. Failure to do so is a criminal offence and may result in legal action against the company and its officers.

- The confirmation statement must be signed by a trustee or the secretary or submitted (as is more common these days) via the web filing service by a registered user.

Conflicts of interest

Introduction

Academy trusts are publicly funded charitable companies. Charity trustees are required to act only in the best interests of the charity and company directors have a statutory duty to avoid conflicts of interest. As public bodies there is a responsibility on all those involved with the trust to act in accordance with the Nolan principles.

Conflicts of interest can be both pecuniary and of loyalty.

It is generally considered good practice for charities to maintain a register of interests of their trustees and senior managers, but it is a requirement of the AFH 2018 and extends to members and those governing at academy level in MATs. The AFH 2018 sets out the rules as to who and what must be declared. These must be published on the trust's or individual academy's website.

The AFH 2018 also has specific rules on how related/connected party transactions must be dealt with. Related party transactions are financial transactions where the academy trust is contracting for goods or services with someone who is closely connected to the trust (e.g. member, trustee or senior executive leader). Any related party transaction with a value of more than £2,500 or a series of transactions over the course of a year which will amount to more than £2,500 must be carried out 'at cost'. From April 2019 all related party transactions with a single or cumulative value of £20,000 must be submitted to the ESFA for approval.

In addition, trustees must declare where they have a conflict of interest in any item on the agenda of a meeting which they are attending.

Academy trusts should have a policy for dealing with conflicts of interest.

Checklist

- Consider the legal and regulatory principles governing conflicts of interest.

- Ensure members, trustees and senior staff understand the principles and rules governing conflicts of interest.

- Adopt a conflicts of interest policy.

▷ Ensure that recruitment procedures for potential members, trustees, and in MATs those governing at academy level include declarations of interests.

▷ Ensure all existing members, trustees, academy committee members and senior staff complete a declaration of interests.

▷ Follow all relevant procedures, i.e. those in the articles, legislation and AFH 2018.

▷ Ensure conflicts of loyalty receive the same consideration as pecuniary interests.

▷ Deal with related party transactions in accordance with the AFH 2018.

▷ Consider the reputational risks to the academy trust of any conflicts, irrespective of whether the conflict is not strictly unlawful.

▷ Publish the register of interests on the website.

Procedure

▷ Request declarations of interest from prospective members, trustees and academy committee members.

▷ Remind existing members, trustees, academy committee members and senior staff to update their declarations of interest annually, but also if anything changes.

▷ Publish the register of interest on the trust's website.

▷ Ensure approval for any qualifying related party transactions are sought from the ESFA.

Filing requirements

▷ Register of interest must be published on the trust's website.

▷ Approval must be sought from the ESFA for qualifying related party transactions.

▷ Related party transactions will need to be recorded in the annual report and accounts.

Notes

▷ Related party transactions have been the subject of considerable interest and controversy in relation to academy trusts. The PAC has raised concerns about these transactions on several occasions. As a result of this scrutiny the ESFA has tightened the rules.

▷ Where possible, it is better to avoid conflicts of interest than to try to manage them. Related party transactions are subject to significant scrutiny and trustees should think very carefully about the reputational risk to the organisation before authorising them. Even where such conflicts have been managed according to strict procedures, it is likely that the prevailing perception will be that those governing the trust are 'benefiting' from their involvement.

▶ The Charity Commission publishes helpful guidance to trustees on conflicts of interest.

More information

▶ Academy Governance Checklists: Related party transactions.

▶ AFH 2018.

▶ DfE *Governance Handbook*.

▶ Charity Commission guidance:

▷ Conflicts of interest: a guide for charity trustees www.gov.uk/government/publications/conflicts-of-interest-a-guide-for-charity-trustees-cc29

▷ It's your decision: charity trustees and decision making www.gov.uk/government/publications/its-your-decision-charity-trustees-and-decision-making

▶ *Academy Governance Handbook*, Chapter 1.

De facto directors/trustees and shadow directors

Introduction

The Charity SORP document describes a de facto trustee as 'a person who has not been validly appointed as a trustee but is acting as the trustee of the charity and is exercising the functions that could only be properly discharged by a trustee. This may have come about due to an error, omission or oversight in the appointment process of that trustee. A trustee who is a de facto trustee of a company charity may alternatively be known as a de facto director.'

In the CA2006 a director is defined as 'any person occupying the position of director, by whatever name called'. In academy trusts, directors are also trustees and may be known as such and in some cases may be referred to as governors.

The Companies Act goes on to define a 'shadow director' as 'a person in accordance with whose directions or instructions the directors of the company are accustomed to act'. There is no definitive test as to whether someone is a shadow director, but case law provides a list of circumstances to be considered.

Legal judgements have distinguished between the two terms – so that a de facto director/trustee is someone 'who claims to act and purports to act as director, although not validly appointed as such' whereas a shadow director 'does not claim or purport to act as director. On the contrary, he claims not to be a director. He lurks in the shadows, sheltering behind others who, he claims, are the only directors of the company to the exclusion of himself.'

Both de facto and shadow directors are subject to the same legal duties, responsibilities and potential liabilities as properly appointed directors.

The AFH 2018 prohibits academy trusts from having de facto trustees or shadow directors.

Checklist

▶ Directors must be properly appointed under the articles of association.

Procedures

▶ Ensure procedures are in place for recruiting, appointing and registering directors.

Notes

▶ Academy trusts have power within their articles of association to appoint non-trustees to committees of the board, providing that the majority of members of the committee are trustees. Such persons have no right to attend meetings of the board. Where such individuals have been appointed the trustees need to be careful to limit their influence to the committees to which they have been appointed and not to treat them as 'directors'.

More information

▶ Academy Governance Checklists:

  ▷ Directors – appointment;
  ▷ Trustee committees.

▶ AFH 2018.

▶ *Academy Governance Handbook*, Chapter 4.

Delegation of authority

Introduction

Academy trustee boards need to determine what powers and functions to retain for themselves and what to delegate to the senior executive lead, committees or individual trustees.

The articles of association give wide powers to the trustees to delegate their powers and functions to the senior executive leader, any trustee, trustee board committee, in MATs academy committees, or any other holder of an executive office. Delegated powers must be recorded in writing and can be revoked or amended by the trustees when and if they see fit.

There are two specific delegation documents required by the AFH 2018. These are:

▶ the scheme of delegation for governance functions (SoD); and

▶ the scheme of delegation of financial powers.

Both must be written schemes, approved by the trustees. The SoD must be published on the academy trust's website. Both should be reviewed and approved annually.

The trustee board needs to determine which decisions are so important that they must be reserved for the board and which can be delegated and to which level. This is more complex in a MAT where there are multiple academies across different sites. The SoD should not be a static document and will almost certainly need to change over time – again this will be especially the case in a MAT, particularly an expanding one.

The trustee board as a corporate entity remains responsible and accountable for all decisions made, whoever they have been delegated to.

Checklist

▶ Must have a written scheme of delegation for governance functions, approved by the trustees.

▶ Must have a written scheme of delegation of financial powers, approved by the trustees.

- The SoD must be published on the academy trust website.

- Ensure the schemes of delegation are properly communicated to all trustees, staff and those on academy committees.

Procedures

- Once a year:

  - the scheme of delegation for governance functions should be an item on the agenda for approval on a properly convened and quorate trustees' meeting; and
  - the scheme of delegation of financial powers should be an item on the agenda for approval at a properly convened and quorate trustees' meeting.

- Arrange for the SoD to be published on the academy trust website.

Notes

- It is for the trustee board to determine when annually to approve the SoD – historically many governing boards used to do this at the first meeting of the academic year, which is also the financial year for academies, but there is also merit in doing this at the last meeting of the academic year, as any new structures are then approved ready for the start of term.

- The board should keep at the forefront of its mind that its role is strategic and reserve only those matters and decisions which fall within that remit. Responsibility for the day-to-day operation and management of the trust should be delegated to the senior executive lead.

- The SoD needs to be as explicit as possible about what power/ function has been delegated and to whom. Lack of clarity in the SoD will lead to at best confusion and at worst decisions that affect the success of the trust. It is particularly important in MATs to ensure there is clear delineation between what powers and functions are delegated to the senior executive leader and what are delegated to the academy committee.

More information

- Academy Governance Checklists:

  - Financial scheme of delegation;
  - Scheme of delegation (of governance functions).

- *Academy Governance Handbook*, Chapter 6 (and 3 and 12).

Department for Education (DfE)

Introduction

The DfE is the government department responsible for education policy in England. The secretary of state for education is legally responsible for all education policy and is the principal regulator of academy trusts.

The DfE is responsible for overseeing education legislation and additionally produces a range of guidance. Guidance comes with varying status: that which must be followed, that which academy trusts need to have regard to and have good reasons for not following, and 'advice' which is for trusts to decide whether to follow. Academy trusts need to be clear which guidance is relevant to them and what status it has.

The DfE is supported by 19 agencies and public bodies – the ones with most direct relevance to academy trusts are Ofsted and the ESFA.

Schools Commissioners Group

Academy trusts' main interaction with the DfE is likely to be via the relevant Regional Schools Commissioner (RSC). RSCs are civil servants based within the DfE. There are eight RSCs, one of whom also acts currently as the Interim National Schools Commissioner. Each RSC is responsible for a specific region of the country – these regions are distinct to the RSCs and do not correspond to regions used by other organisations (e.g. Ofsted). MATs may well have dealings with more than one RSC.

The RSCs are responsible for approving new academies, changes to existing ones and monitoring the education performance of academy trusts and intervening in poorly performing trusts. They work closely with the ESFA.

RSCs are advised and supported by headteacher boards (HTBs). The HTB members are non-executive although remunerated; the members' role is to provide advice, scrutiny and challenge to the RSC's decision-making. Decisions are ultimately for the RSCs to take, but they should be informed by the views of their HTB.

All academy funding agreements set out the terms on which the Secretary of State for education can intervene in the academy trust on performance grounds. For MATs these grounds are set out in the supplementary funding agreement for each of the academies in the MAT. These powers are generally exercised by the RSCs on behalf of the secretary of state.

Where the education performance of an academy is a cause for concern, the RSC has the power to issue a pre-warning or a warning notice. Where the RSC is not satisfied that a trust has the capacity to improve then it has the power to terminate the funding agreement. In MATs this is can be for the supplementary funding agreement for an individual academy, which will then be rebrokered to another trust, but in extremis could be the Master funding agreement.

Checklist

▷ The Secretary of State is the principal regulator of academy trusts.

▷ The DfE has powers of intervention in academy trusts in specified circumstances.

▷ The DfE publishes a range of guidance and advice which trusts should keep abreast of.

Filing requirements

▷ Academy trusts are required to place information about their trust on the DfE's GIAS website.

More information

▷ Academy Governance Checklists: Principal regulator.

▷ DfE General.

▷ DfE Schools Commissioners Office.

▷ ESFA.

▷ *Academy Governance Handbook*, Chapter 2.

Directors – appointment

Introduction

Academy trusts are charitable companies; those sitting on the board have dual roles as company directors and charity trustees.

The appointment methods for both directors and trustees will be the same, i.e. in accordance with the articles of association. (For the detailed process, see Trustees – appointment, page 286.)

Companies House needs to be notified about the appointment of directors.

Checklist

▶ Check articles of association for any trust-specific eligibility rules for director appointments.

▶ Check articles of association to establish who has the authority to appoint directors.

▶ Is the proposed director at least 18 years old?

▶ Is the director disqualified from acting by statute or the articles of association?

▶ Obtain written consent from the individual to be appointed as a director.

Procedure

▶ Follow the academy trust's director/trustee recruitment procedure.

▶ Parent trustees – arrange an election in line with the articles and any rules adopted by the academy trust.

▶ Staff trustee – follow the procedures set out in the articles/adopted by the trust (current model articles do not allow for elected staff trustees, but some earlier versions do).

▶ Convene meeting of members/directors depending on which category of director is being appointed.

▷ File completed APO1 form at Companies House.

▷ Update the trust's records via the governance portal on the DfE's GIAS website.

Filing requirements

▷ Form AP01 at Companies House within 14 days of appointment.

▷ Notify the ESFA via the governance portal of GIAS.

More information

▷ Academy Governance Checklists:

  ▷ Trustees – appointment;
  ▷ Trustees – recruitment.

▷ *Academy Governance Handbook*, Chapter 4.

Directors – cessation of office

Introduction

It is considered best practice for there to be turnover on any board, to prevent it getting stale or 'cosy'. Articles of association will stipulate a term of office for a director (usually three/four years) but will often also include a maximum length of service, precisely to facilitate turnover. Academy trust articles have four-year terms of office, but no maximum length of service. It is open to the trustee board to introduce its own rules about relating to maximum length of service. The National Governance Association recommends that generally directors should not serve more than two four-year terms of office.

A director may cease to hold office for a variety of reasons. They:

▶ may resign – under the model articles a director can resign at any point, providing there remain at least three directors in office;

▶ may come to the end of the term of office – the model articles provide for a four-year term of office. The model articles do not contain a maximum length of service so directors can be re-elected or reappointed at the end of the four-year term, unless the trustee board has adopted its own maximum;

▶ may be disqualified from further service as a director – the Company Directors Disqualification Act 1986 sets out the circumstances in which a director can be disqualified (see Disqualification rules, page 124).

▶ may be removed from office by:

  ▷ the person who appointed them – a director may be removed at any time by the person/persons who appointed them; or
  ▷ the members – the members of the academy trust have the power to remove any director by means of an ordinary resolution; this includes elected directors.

Checklist

▶ Check the articles of association for the rules about removal of directors.

▷ Written notice must be given to the clerk to the trustees where the trustee resigns or is removed from office.

▷ Companies House must be informed via form TM01 within 14 days.

▷ The ESFA must be informed using the governance portal of GIAS.

▷ The register of directors must be updated.

Procedure

Resignation

▷ It is best practice to obtain a written letter of resignation.

▷ The clerk to the trustee board must be informed in writing of the resignation.

▷ Ensure the resignation is noted in the minutes of the next relevant meeting.

▷ The ESFA will need to be notified via Get Information about Schools – within 14 days.

▷ Companies House need to be informed by TM01 within 14 days.

▷ The relevant registers will need to be amended.

▷ Update the trust's website and any other relevant material.

Removal from office

▷ It is generally better to seek the resignation of a director than to use formal removal procedures.

Procedure – removal by an individual or other body entitled to appoint a trustee

▷ The person or company must write to the clerk informing them of the removal of the trustee.

▷ Minutes of the next trustees meeting should record the removal.

▷ ESFA should be notified via Get Information about Schools.

▷ Companies House should be informed using form TM01.

Procedure – removal at a board meeting of a director appointed by the board

▷ The articles do not provide a set process for carrying out this procedure.

▷ Removal requires a formal vote so it should be a stated item of business on the agenda of a meeting.

▷ Convene a meeting of the directors.

▷ Quorum for a meeting at which it is proposed to remove a director is in the model articles two-thirds shall be any two-thirds (rounded up to a whole number) of the persons who are at the time Trustees present at the meeting and entitled to vote on those respective trustees matters.

▷ The director proposed for removal should be given the opportunity to respond to the resolution.

▷ Resolution requires a simple majority.

▷ The clerk to the trustee board must be informed in writing of the removal.

▷ Notify the ESFA within 14 days via the governance portal of GIAS.

▷ Companies House should be informed using TMO1.

Procedure – removal by the members

▷ The members have the power to remove any director of the company by virtue of an ordinary resolution. A director can only be removed at a meeting – i.e. not by written resolution.

▷ Special notice must be given to the company of the proposal to remove a director – notice can be given by the Company Secretary or director. Special notices must be issued 28 clear days before the meeting.

▷ A copy of the special notice must be sent to the director whose removal is proposed.

▷ If necessary, convene general meeting of members giving 14 clear days notice. The notice of the general meeting should specify that special notice has been given. The director proposed for removal is entitled to have written representation circulated with the notice.

▷ A simple majority is required to carry the proposal.

▷ If resolution is approved file form TM01 with Companies House.

▷ The register of directors must be updated.

▷ The ESFA must be notified within 14 days via the GIAS website.

Other cessations of office

▷ Most of the steps set out under the resignation procedure will apply.

Filing requirements

▷ Form TMO1 to Companies House within 14 days.

▷ ESFA via GIAS within 14 days.

More information

▷ Academy Governance Checklists: Disqualification rules (for members, trustees, directors and those on academy committees).

▷ *Academy Governance Handbook*, Chapter 4.

Directors – duties

Introduction

All those sitting on the trustee board of an academy trust are both charity trustees and company directors.

Checklist

Directors' statutory duties are to:

- act within powers – must act in accordance with the articles of association and only exercise powers for the purpose of which they were conferred;

- promote the success of the company – a director must act in a way they consider in good faith would be most likely to promote the success of the company;

- exercise independent judgement;

- exercise reasonable care, skill and diligence – in practice this means that a director is expected to exercise the same care and skill that would be exercised by a reasonably diligent person with:

  - ▷ the same general knowledge skill and experience that may reasonable be expected of a person carrying out the same functions as a director; and
  - ▷ the specific general knowledge, skill and experience of the particular director;

- avoid conflicts of interest – directors must avoid situations in which they have a conflict of interest (see also Related party transactions, page 245);

- not to accept benefits from third parties – directors must not accept any benefits given by a third party which are given purely because of their position as a director; and

- declare any interest in a proposed transaction or arrangement – directors are required to declare any interest, direct or indirect, in any transaction (see also Conflicts of interest, page 104, and Register of interests, members, trustees/directors, academy committees and staff, page 238).

Filing requirements

▶ Academy trusts are required to maintain a register of interests of all directors and this must be published on the trust's website.

Notes

▶ In academy trusts, the directors' duties need also to be considered in line with their duties as charity trustees which are similar but distinct. They are also bound by the rules governing public bodies – in particular, the Nolan principles.

More information

▶ Academy Governance Checklists:

▷ Conflicts of interest;
▷ Register of interests, members, trustees/directors, academy committees and staff;
▷ Trustees – duties.

▶ Companies House Guidance Booklet GP3.

▶ *Academy Governance Handbook*, Chapter 4.

Disclosure and Barring Service checks

Introduction

The Disclosure and Barring Service (DBS) is responsible for overseeing criminal records checks as well as specific lists (barred lists) which prevent people from working in certain sectors.

Any employees working in academy trusts in what is classed as 'regulated activity' must have an enhanced disclosure with barring check.

The Education (Independent School Standards) Regulations 2014, the model articles of association, the funding agreement and the DfE's statutory safeguarding guidance *Keeping Children Safe in Education* (KCSIE) all contain provisions about the level of checks required on those governing in academy trusts. The problem is that the documents are not consistent, and it can be difficult to be sure about the correct level of checks. As with other issues, different versions of articles of associations contain slightly different provisions in relation to DBS checks.

Members, trustees and those governing at academy committee level in MATs are required to undergo enhanced DBS checks. The chair of the trustees is additionally required to have their DBS check counter-signed by the Secretary of State.

The Secretary of State also has the power under s. 128 of the Education and Skills Act 2008 to prohibit a person from taking part in the management of an independent school, including academies and free schools – this would prohibit an individual from being a trustee of an academy trust. Trustees should be checked against this register.

Checklist

▶ Enhanced DBS and barring list checks must be carried out on all employees engaged in regulated activity – in practice, there will be very few employees not covered by this provision.

▶ Enhanced DBS checks must be carried out on existing trustees (where these are not already held), prospective members, trustees and in MATs those at academy committee level.

▶ Check members, trustees and those at academy committee level (if the level of delegation to the committee gives them management responsibilities) against the s. 128 list.

▶ Trustees are disqualified from taking up or continuing in office if they refuse to provide an enhanced DBS certificate.

▶ Trustees can also be disqualified if the DBS certificate discloses information which in the opinion of the senior executive leader and/ or chair confirms their unsuitability to work with children.

Procedure

▶ Ensure appropriate procedures are in place for all employees to receive the appropriate level of DBS check.

▶ Ensure that there are processes in place for all new trustees and those governing at academy committee level to undergo appropriate DBS and s. 128 checks.

Filing requirements

▶ All academy trusts are required to maintain a Single Central Record (SCR), which lists all employees, members and trustees. Against each individual the SCR should indicate what checks have been done and when. The relevant checks are:

▷ an identity check;
▷ a barred list check;
▷ an enhanced DBS check/certificate;
▷ a prohibition from teaching check;
▷ further checks on people who have lived or worked outside the UK;
▷ a check of professional qualifications, where required;
▷ a check to establish the person's right to work in the UK; and
▷ a s. 128 check (for management positions in academy trusts).

More information

▶ Academy Governance Checklists: Chair of trustees – role and responsibilities.

▶ DfE:

▷ *Governance Handbook 2019*: www.gov.uk/government/publications/governance-handbook
▷ KCSIE: www.gov.uk/government/publications/keeping-children-safe-in-education—2

▶ Academy articles of association.

▶ The Education (Independent School Standards) Regulations 2014.

▶ *Academy Governance Handbook*, Chapter 8.

Disclosure requirements

Introduction

Academy trusts as charitable companies are subject to the Company, Limited Liability Partnership and Business (Names and Trading Disclosures) Regulations 2015 (SI 2015/17). In addition, the DfE and ESFA require certain information to be published on the trust's website.

Company requirements

Specifically, these relate to the publication of the company's name, company number, registered office address and, where registered on certain documents, website and premises. Any information published must be in legible characters.

Checklist

▶ On business letters, order forms, orders for goods and services and the company website – all four items must be displayed. In MATs this information must also appear on the websites of academies within the MAT.

▶ On cheques, invoices and receipts, notices and official publications, letters of credit, written demands for payment of debts and applications for licences to carry on a trade or activity, the company name only is required.

▶ Company name – charitable companies that have been granted permission to omit 'limited' must state that they are limited companies.

▶ The company name must also be displayed at:

   ▷ the company's registered office;
   ▷ any inspection place – i.e. any location other than the registered office where it keeps records available for public inspection;
   ▷ every location at which the company carries on business that is not the registered office or an inspection place.

Requirements specific to academy trusts

▶ All schools are required to upload information and documentation on their websites.

▶ The model funding agreement requires the following to be uploaded:

▷ funding agreement, memorandum and articles of association;
▷ the annual report and accounts;
▷ the names of the trustees;
▷ the names of the members; and
▷ the trust's current articles of association.

▶ The website must include:

▷ the name of the academy;
▷ postal address;
▷ telephone number;
▷ name of the member of staff who deals with queries from parents and other members of the public;
▷ name of the headteacher or principal;
▷ name and address of the chair of the governing board;
▷ name and details of the special educational needs co-ordinator (SENCo) if it is a mainstream academy;
▷ sponsor; and
▷ the admission arrangements (which must be compliant with the School Admissions Code and School Admission Appeals Code), which must be published and kept on the website for the full duration of the offer year. Alternatively, details should be provided of how the arrangements may be obtained through the local authority.

▶ If the trust is sponsored, the website should contain information about:

▷ the full name and contact details (address and a telephone number) where the sponsor is an individual;
▷ the address and telephone number of the office where the sponsor is a group or organisation; and
▷ admissions.

Filing requirements

None.

More information

▶ *Academy Governance Handbook*, Chapter 9.

Disqualification rules (for members, trustees, directors and those on academy committees)

Introduction

There are specific provisions in company law, charity law, education legislation and the articles of association which prohibit an individual from taking up or continuing to act as a member or director/trustee of an academy trust – and in some cases from sitting on an academy committee.

Disqualification rules for trustees, non-trustee members of trust committee and academy committee members

The model articles of association stipulate that individuals are disqualified from acting or continuing to act as a trustee, a trust committee member or a member of an academy committee if they:

▸ are aged under 18;

▸ have a pupil/student at the academy or one of the academies run by the trust;

▸ become incapable by reason of illness or injury of managing or administering their own affairs;

▸ are absent without the permission of the trustees from all their meetings held within a period of six months and the trustees resolve that their office be vacated;

▸ have been declared bankrupt and/or their estate has been seized from their possession for the benefit of their creditors and the declaration or seizure has not been discharged, annulled or reduced; or

▸ are subject to a disqualification order or a disqualification undertaking under the Company Directors Disqualification Act 1986 or to an order made under s. 429(2)(b) of the Insolvency Act 1986 (failure to pay under county court administration order);

▸ cease to be a trustee by virtue of any provision in the CA2006, or are disqualified from acting as a trustee by virtue of s. 178 of the Charities Act 2011 (or any statutory re-enactment or modification of that provision);

▸ have been removed from the office of charity trustee or trustee for a charity by an order made by the Charity Commission or the High

Court on the grounds of any misconduct or mismanagement in the administration of the charity for which they were responsible or to which they were privy, or which they by their conduct contributed to or facilitated;

▶ have at any time, been convicted of any criminal offence, excluding any that have been spent under the Rehabilitation of Offenders Act 1974 as amended, and excluding any offence for which the maximum sentence is a fine or a lesser sentence except where a person has been convicted of any offence which falls under s. 178 of the Charities Act 2011; or

▶ have not provided to the chairman of the trustees a criminal records certificate at an enhanced disclosure level under s. 113B of the Police Act 1997 after the trust has opened or the certificate indicates that in the opinion of the chair or senior executive leader they are unsuitable to work with children.

Disqualification rules for members

Members of academy trusts must undergo an enhanced Disclosure and Barring service check and a s. 128 check – which might lead to them being prevented from taking up office as member.

Checklist

▶ Recruitment documentation should contain the disqualification criteria.

▶ Eligibility checks must be carried out on all prospective: trustees, non-trustee committee members and academy committee members.

▶ Any trustee who meets the disqualification threshold is required to write to the clerk to the board and inform them.

Procedure

▶ All prospective trustees, non-trustee committee members and academy committee members should be requested to sign a declaration of eligibility.

▶ All prospective candidates should be checked against the disqualified director (Companies House) and removed trustee (Charity Commission) databases.

▶ All must undergo an enhanced Disclosure and Barring Service check and a s. 128 check.

▶ If an existing trustee/director becomes disqualified Companies House and ESFA will need to be informed.

▶ The register of directors will need to be updated.

Filing requirements

▶ If an existing trustee becomes disqualified and ceases to be a trustee – form TM01 to Companies House – within 14 days.

▶ ESFA to be informed via GIAS within 14 days.

Education and Skills Funding Agency (ESFA)

Introduction

The ESFA is an executive agency of the DfE and is accountable for funding education and skills for children, young people and adults. It is responsible for regulating academies on behalf of the Secretary of State (who is the principal regulator). It has powers of intervention where there is a risk of failure or evidence of mismanagement of public funds.

Checklist

Role of the ESFA in relation to academy trusts

▶ The Chief Executive of the ESFA, as AO, is responsible for safeguarding the public funds for which the ESFA has charge; for ensuring propriety, regularity, value for money and feasibility in the handling of those public funds; and for the day-to-day operations and management of the ESFA.

ESFA guidance

▶ The ESFA publishes the AFH, which is updated annually. Academy trusts are required by their funding agreements to follow the requirements contained in the AFH and have regard to its guidance.

▶ The chief executive of the ESFA sends an annual letter to academy trusts' AOs. The letter reminds AOs of their overall responsibilities, but also highlights any areas of concern the ESFA has across the academy sector (in recent years these have covered related party transactions and executive pay). The annual letter is usually sent close to the start of the academy trust financial year. Additional letters are sent during the year if the ESFA needs to draw attention to new requirements. Letters to accounting officers must be shared with members, trustees, the CFO and senior leadership team.

Intervention powers

▶ The ESFA has the power to issue financial notices to improve (FNtI), to trusts where it has concerns about financial management or governance.

▶ Trusts must comply with terms of an FNtI. Failure to comply is a breach of the funding agreement and could lead to termination of the funding agreement.

Financial returns

Academy trusts are required to submit several returns to the ESFA. These are:

▶ accounts return;

▶ annual report and accounts;

▶ budget forecast return;

▶ budget forecast return (outturn); and

▶ land and buildings collection tool.

Filing requirements

▶ The financial returns listed above.

▶ Information about those governing in the trust (members, trustees, academy committee members), accounting officer and chief financial officer via GIAS.

More information

▶ *Academy Governance Handbook*, Chapter 2.

Exclusions – general

Introduction

Exclusion is the technical term for when a pupil is prohibited from attending the school either for a fixed term or permanently. Only the headteacher/principal or acting headteacher/principal can exclude a pupil and only on behavioural grounds.

Exclusion, particularly permanent exclusion, should be a last resort.

The Education (Independent School Standard) Regulations require all academy trusts to have a written behaviour policy which sets out the expected standards of behaviour and the sanctions that will apply where pupils do not meet those standards.

Permanent exclusions must meet two tests to be legal:

▷ in response to a serious breach, or persistent breaches, of the school's behaviour policy; and

▷ where allowing the pupil to remain in school would seriously harm the education or welfare of the pupil or others in the school.

Checklist

▷ Ensure there is an agreed behaviour policy which sets out expected standards of behaviour and sanctions.

Filing requirements

▷ Behaviour policy should be published on the academy trust and individual academy websites.

Exclusions – trustees' role

Introduction

The trustee board has a specific role in relation to exclusions. Only the principal/acting principal can make an exclusion, but certain exclusion decisions must be reviewed by the trustee board. The trustee board can delegate their review responsibilities to the relevant academy committee.

Where a trustee board is required to review an exclusion decision, it must be lawful, reasonable and procedurally fair.

Checklist

The trustee board must review:

- any fixed term exclusion if requested to do so by the parents of the pupil concerned:
  - review must take place within 50 days;
  - trustee board has no power to over-turn the decision;

- any fixed term exclusion which would mean that a pupil has been excluded for more than 15 days in a single term:
  - review should take place within 15 days of the exclusion;
  - if the exclusion would cause a pupil to miss a public exam every effort should be made to hold the review before the exam.

- all permanent exclusions:
  - review should take place within 15 days of the exclusion;
  - trustee board can uphold or over-turn the decision.

- In a MAT ensure that exclusions are appropriately delegated (if exclusions are not delegated to academy committee level then the trustees remain responsible for undertaking reviews – in a large MAT this will be difficult).

- Ensure parents are informed how they can appeal about any decisions to exclude.

- Ensure all exclusion panels are properly clerked.

- Ensure all panel members have received appropriate training.

Procedure

▶ Where appropriate, delegation of exclusions to be included in the SoD.

▶ In a SAT or in a MAT where exclusions are not delegated, agree a panel for hearing exclusion reviews.

▶ Arrange exclusion panel training for all those who will sit on review panels.

▶ Arrange panel hearing as necessary.

▶ Issue decision letter to parents – include details of how to appeal to an independent review panel.

▶ Where a decision is made to permanently exclude, the pupil must be removed from the school register.

Independent Review Panel (IRP)

▶ Establish an independent review panel in accordance with the School Discipline (Pupil Exclusions and Reviews) (England) Regulations 2012.

Review following a decision by the IRP

▶ Where the IRP:

▷ quashes the decision and directs the governing board to reconsider reinstatement; or
▷ recommends that the governing board reconsiders reinstatement.

▶ Convene a panel to reconsider the exclusion.

▶ Inform the parents of the decision.

Exclusions – academy committee's role

In a MAT where the trustee board has delegated responsibility for hearing exclusions appeals to the AC then its role is to carry out the function of the trustee board and hold panels when necessary.

Executive headteacher

Introduction

All academy trusts must have a senior executive leader. What this person is called will depend on the size and circumstances of the trust.

The generally accepted definition of an executive headteacher is an individual who runs more than one school. In smaller MATs this person might also be the senior executive leader. However, in larger MATs there may be a chief executive and then one or more executive headteachers.

More information

- Academy Governance Checklists:

  - Accounting officer;
  - Chief executive officer;
  - Principal;
  - Senior executive leader.

Exempt charity status

Introduction

All academy trusts are charitable companies and are exempt charities. This means that they do not need to register with the Charity Commission and instead are regulated by a 'principal regulator'. The principal regulator for academies is the Secretary of State for Education, whose responsibilities are carried out by the DfE and the ESFA.

Being a charity carries specific legal responsibilities in the way its funds and assets are managed. This is true whether the organisation is a registered charity, or an exempt charity, such as academy trusts.

Exempt charities are subject to charity law and must have regard to guidance issued by the Charity Commission for England and Wales. Charity status confers certain duties and obligations on those running the organisation.

To be a charity in England or Wales, the organisation must be set up with purposes which are exclusively charitable for the public benefit.

The Charities Act 2011 describes a charitable purpose as one which falls within 13 definitions of purposes. All academy trusts have as one of their objects the advancement of education – some trusts have additional objects.

Checklist

▶ The academy trust must pursue its own charitable purpose (as set out in the articles of association) and must do so for the public benefit.

▶ The funds and assets must be protected and used correctly, towards the charitable purposes of the academy trust an in accordance with charity law restrictions and requirements.

▶ No significant private or commercial benefits must arise from the academy trust's activities (any such benefits must be only those that are necessary and incidental to the pursuit of charitable objects).

▶ The academy trust is regulated by charity law and overseen by the relevant charity regulator (e.g. the DfE/ESFA).

▷ The academy trust is publicly accountable and must provide detailed annual accounts and an annual trustees' report.

▷ The members have no commercial interest – they do not 'own' the charity in the way that the members of a commercial company do.

▷ The trustees are stewards and custodians with legal duties.

Notes

▷ Exempt charities are still subject to charity law.

More information

▷ Academy Governance Checklists:

  ▷ Charitable status;
  ▷ Charity Commission for England and Wales;
  ▷ Department for Education (DfE);
  ▷ Education and Skills Funding Agency (ESFA);
  ▷ Principal regulator.

▷ *Academy Governance Handbook*, Chapter 2.

Finance Committee

Introduction

The model articles of association for academy trusts give trustees freedom to determine how they manage their business, including whether to establish any committees.

This freedom is slightly fettered by the AFH 2018. A condition of the model funding agreement is that academy trusts, in relation to any grant paid must follow any requirements of the AFH and otherwise have regard to its guidance.

The AFH 2018 states that the 'academy trust should have a finance committee to which the board delegates financial scrutiny and oversight'. While this is a 'should' not 'must' the academy trust will need to show good reason if it chooses not to operate a finance committee.

Checklist

▷ AFH guidance is that trusts should have a finance committee.

▷ Model articles of association require that the terms of reference and membership of any committee must be reviewed annually.

▷ Trustee committees may have non-trustees appointed to them provided the majority of committee members are trustees. Decisions will only be valid if a majority of the committee present and voting are trustees.

▷ All decisions taken by a committee must be reported to the next meeting of trustees – this is usually done by way of the minutes of the committee meeting.

Procedure

▷ Convene a trustees' meeting to determine membership and terms of reference for the committee – this is usually done at the first full meeting of the trustees in the autumn term.

▷ Agree how the committee chair will be determined – i.e. will the trustees appoint, or delegate this to the committee.

▷ Committee membership and terms of reference should form part of the SoD – detailed decision-making powers should be cross-referenced to the written scheme of delegation of financial powers.

▷ Financial decision making power will need to be recorded in the written scheme of delegation of financial powers.

▷ Minutes of meeting to be included as agenda items for next full trustees' meeting.

Filing requirements

▷ Decisions made by the finance committee must be reported to the full board of trustees at its next meeting – usually by way of the minutes of the committee meeting.

More information

▷ Academy Governance Checklists:

▷ Academies Financial Handbook;
▷ Articles of association – general;
▷ Financial scheme of delegation;
▷ Scheme of delegation (of governance functions).

▷ *Academy Governance Handbook*, Chapter 6.

Financial Notice to Improve

Introduction

The ESFA has powers of intervention in academy trusts where it has concerns about the governance or financial management of the trust. Where it has serious concerns the ESFA can issue a Financial Notice to Improve (FNtI). Trusts are required by the AFH 2018 to comply with a FNtI and a failure to do so classes as a breach of the funding agreement and could lead to the termination of that agreement.

The FNtI will set out the basis of the ESFA's concerns and the steps the academy trust must take in order to remedy the situation. In some cases, the ESFA will restrict the academy trust's ability to make financial decisions without its prior approval.

Checklist

▶ The trust must comply with the requirements set out in an FNtI.

▶ FNtIs are published on the ESFA's website.

▶ Inability or failure to comply with the FNtI may lead to termination of the academy trust's funding agreement.

Procedure

▶ The ESFA will issue an FNtI to the chair of the trust.

▶ The trustees must provide an action plan of how they will meet the requirements of the FNtI.

▶ The ESFA will monitor progress:

▷ if it is not satisfied it may issue a termination warning notice; or
▷ if it is satisfied the FNtI will be revoked.

Filing requirements

▶ The academy trust will be required to keep the ESFA updated on progress towards complying with the FNtI; this might include sending regular budget reports.

Notes

▷ The ESFA generally issues an FNtI only after other less formal forms of intervention have been unsuccessful. It is an indication of serious problems in the financial management and governance of a trust.

▷ Where the ESFA indicates to a trust that it has concerns, the trustees should take immediate advice and action in order to prevent the need for an FNtI. Where concerns are raised trustees should consider whether they need additional expertise on the trustee board and/or additional professional expertise on the staff team.

More information

▷ Academy Governance Checklists: Education and Skills Funding Agency (ESFA).

▷ *Academy Governance Handbook*, Chapter 12.

Financial scheme of delegation

Introduction

The AFH 2018 requires that all academy trusts have a written scheme of delegation of financial powers in order to maintain 'robust internal control arrangements'. This is separate to the scheme of delegation for governance functions (SoD), although the two should cross-refer.

Checklist

▸ All academy trusts must have a written scheme of delegation of financial powers for managing internal control – reviewed and agreed annually.

▸ The AFH describes internal controls as procedures which:

  ▷ ensure delegated financial authorities are complied with – the scheme of financial delegation should stipulate:
- who is authorised to approve expenditure (e.g. senior executive leader, committee or trustee board);
- to what value;
- any procurement rules – e.g. necessity of obtaining three quotes;

  ▷ maintain appropriate segregation of duties; and
  ▷ ensure the same person is not approving expenditure and making payments.

Procedure

▸ Convene a trustees' meeting to approve the written scheme of delegation of financial powers – this must be done annually.

▸ Written scheme of delegation of financial powers must be communicated to all those governing or working in the trust.

▸ Ensure the SoD is cross-referenced to the financial scheme of delegation.

▸ Establish internal mechanisms to ensure the written scheme of delegation of financial powers is being properly implemented.

Filing requirements

▶ The academy trust must have a written scheme of financial delegation – this does not need to be published on the trust's website but may be.

Notes

▶ Charity law requires that trustees both act in the best interests of their charity and manage the charity's resources responsibly. This means the trustee board must:

  ▷ make sure the charity's assets are only used to support or carry out its purposes;
  ▷ avoid exposing the charity's assets, beneficiaries or reputation to undue risk;
  ▷ not over-commit the charity;
  ▷ take special care when investing or borrowing;
  ▷ comply with any restrictions on spending funds or selling land; and
  ▷ ideally put appropriate procedures and safeguards in place and take reasonable steps to ensure that these are followed to reduce the risk of exposing the charity and potentially being in breach of its charitable duties.

More information

▶ Academy Governance Checklists:

  ▷ Academies Financial Handbook;
  ▷ Financial scheme of delegation;
  ▷ Trustees – duties.

Free schools

Introduction

Free schools are a type of academy. Free schools are brand new schools set up from scratch as opposed to maintained schools who convert to academy status. The 'free school' moniker also encompasses studio schools and UTCs.

Any brand new academy, whether it is established to provide additional school places in areas of shortage or proposed to increase educational choice in an area, is known as a free school. Local authorities are not able to open new community schools and where they identify a need for additional school places must run a competition for an organisation to open one.

The then Secretary of State Michael Gove envisaged when he introduced his policy that free schools would be mainly opened by parents or teachers seeking to improve choice in an area. Since 2010 fewer and fewer free schools have been opened in this manner, possibly because of the sheer amount of work required to open any new school. A significant number of free schools are now proposed and established by existing academy trusts.

Checklist

▶ The trustee board must be involved in any decision to propose a free school.

▶ As with any expansion of the organisation, full due diligence of the rewards and risks should be carried out.

▶ Academy trusts cannot be forced to take on responsibility for additional schools or establish a free school.

▶ Applications to open a free school will be considered by the RSCs.

Procedure

▶ If the academy trust wishes to set up a free school it should follow the procedure set out on the DfE's website: www.gov.uk/government/collections/opening-a-free-school

▷ It is sensible to have early discussions with the RSC.

More information

▷ Academy Governance Checklists:

> Studio schools;
> University Technical Colleges.

▷ DfE website: www.gov.uk/types-of-school/free-schools

▷ *Academy Governance Handbook*, Chapter 3.

Freedom of Information Act (FOI Act)

Introduction

As public authorities all academy trusts are subject to the Freedom of Information Act 2000 (FOI Act) (Schedule 1 part 4).

The FOI Act places two key duties on academy trusts:

▶ to make available on request any information not covered by one of the exemptions set out in the Act; and

▶ to have a publication scheme setting out what information is routinely available and publish that information. The publication scheme only covers broad headings of information.

Checklist

▶ Ensure someone is responsible for FOI requests.

▶ Adopt the ICO's model publication scheme.

▶ You should publish the publication scheme on your website.

▶ Produce a guide to information specifying what information is available and, where applicable, at what cost. You should also publish this on the website. The ICO has produced an information guide relevant to the sector: https://ico.org.uk/media/for-organisations/documents/1235/definition-document-schools-in-england.pdf

▶ You should publish information about how to request information and if you refuse to provide information how to appeal against that decision.

▶ Respond to other FOI requests within legal guidelines: 20 working days or 60 school days.

Procedure

▶ Ensure that an appropriate member of staff is designated to receive FOI requests.

▶ Adopt the model publication scheme – this can be delegated.

▶ Ensure relevant information is published on the academy trust website.

▷ In MATs some information will need to be published on the websites of individual academies.

Filing requirements

▶ The publication scheme should be available on the website.

Notes

▶ Model articles of association, the model funding agreement and the AFH all make stipulations about what information academy trusts must publish on their (or their constituent academies') website(s). This is separate and in addition to FOI requirements. Even if there is not an existing requirement to make information publicly available it can be requested.

▶ The model articles of association require that agendas, minutes and papers of trustee meetings are made available for inspection by any person on request, unless those papers refer to an individual member of staff or pupil or have been declared confidential by the trustees. This latter category holds a very specific meaning under the FOI Act, so unless the information meets that definition or one of the other exemptions in the FOI Act it may still have to be released on request.

More information

▶ Academy Governance Checklists: General Data Protection Regulations.

▶ Information Commissioner's Office: ico.org.uk/for-organisations/guide-to-freedom-of-information

▶ Cabinet Office, Freedom of Information, Code of practice for public authorities: assets.publishing.service.gov.uk/government/uploads/system/uploads/attachment_data/file/744071/CoP_FOI_Code_of_Practice_-_Minor_Amendments_20180926_.pdf

▶ *Academy Governance Handbook*, Chapter 8.

Funding agreement – master

Introduction

All academy trusts have a funding agreement. It is the contract which gives the academy trust the right to run an academy. It is signed by the first members of the academy trust and the DfE on behalf of the Secretary of State. In essence, the contract states that providing the academy trust meets the requirements in the funding agreement the Secretary of State will fund the trust.

SATs have a single funding agreement whereas MATs have a master funding agreement and supplementary funding agreements (see page 148) for each individual academy in their trust.

The DfE has a model funding agreement on its website which, with very few exceptions, is signed unamended by new trusts.

The funding agreement sets out the obligations of both the academy trust and the DfE. It lists the requirements on the academy trust in relation to governance, financial management, educational provision, land and provision of access or information to DfE officials. It then sets out what funding the DfE will provide and how this will be paid.

The funding agreement also sets out the grounds for terminating the contract, by either signatory.

Checklist

▷ All academy trusts sign a funding agreement.

▷ The academy trust must meet the requirements in the funding agreement.

▷ Any breach of the funding agreement could lead to its termination and the wind-up of the trust.

▷ Trustees, senior executive leaders and the governance professional should all familiarise themselves with the funding agreement – the model funding agreement has been amended over time so not all trusts will have an identical agreement.

Academy trust obligations

▶ Governance and management:

▷ including the need to inform and in some cases obtain DfE agreement to changes of members and trustees;

▷ articles of association – funding agreement stipulates trusts must get DfE approval for any changes;

▷ AFH – it is the funding agreement which stipulates that trusts must comply with the AFH.

▶ Educational provision:

▷ freedom to set the length of the school day and year;

▷ curriculum – freedom to determine, but must be broad and balanced;

▷ assessment – requirement that academies are subject to the same assessment regime as maintained schools;

▷ grant funding may only be used to offer qualifications approved by the Secretary of State.

▶ Teachers and staff – freedom to set pay and conditions, although requirement to provide access to the Teachers' Pension Scheme or Local Government Pension Scheme.

▶ School meals – obligation to provide school meals in line with statutory regulations for maintained schools.

▶ Exclusions – sets out obligations in relation to excluded pupils.

▶ Financial management and reporting:

▷ pupil premium – sets out the information which must be published on the trust's website – this is one clause which earlier versions of the model funding agreement did not contain;

▷ charging – obligation for academy trusts to follow the same regulations as maintained schools when charging for school activities;

▷ financial management – sets out the obligations in relation to budgeting, financial management and monitoring and reporting.

▶ Land clauses – sets out obligations in relation to management and disposal.

▶ Complaints – set outs how complaints received before and after the establishment of the trust should be dealt with.

▶ Publication of information – the agreement contains the requirement to publish information under the headings above.

DfE obligations

▶ To pay recurrent expenditure grants.

▶ General Annual Grant (GAG) – DfE will calculate this annually and notify the academy trust before the start of its financial year.

GAG provides the main revenue funding for day-to-day running costs (see General Annual Grant, page 152).

▶ The grant will be paid in monthly instalments.

▶ Publication – the funding agreement must be published on the academy trust's website.

Dual obligations

▶ Termination – either party may give at least seven financial years' notice to terminate, though the secretary of state has significant powers to terminate where there are performance or financial issues.

Procedure

▶ The first members must sign the funding agreement with the DfE – this gives legal permission to run an academy school(s).

Notes

▶ The funding agreement is the legal contract between the trust and the DfE failure to abide by any of its provisions could lead to a warning notice or termination of the agreement. It is critical that those running the trust are familiar with their obligations under the agreement and have mechanisms in place to ensure compliance.

▶ The DfE has revised the model funding agreement several times; if you are working across more than one trust make sure you check the specific document for that trust.

▶ Where an existing trust is taking on a new school the DfE will usually request that they also adopt the latest version of the master funding agreement at the same time.

More information

▶ Academy Governance Checklists:

▷ Funding agreement – supplementary;
▷ Funding agreement – termination.

▶ Funding agreement – for your own trust.

▶ *Academy Governance Handbook*, Chapter 11.

Funding agreement – supplementary

Introduction

MATs have a master funding agreement and supplementary funding agreements for each of the academies they run.

Supplementary agreements are specific to individual academy schools and reflect their characteristics.

Checklist

▷ Supplementary agreements must be read in conjunction with the master funding agreement.

▷ There are different supplementary agreements for: alternative provision, mainstream, special academies and 16–19 academies.

Supplementary agreements details

▷ Pupils – sets out the capacity and age range of the school.

▷ Predecessor school: all pupils at the predecessor school have an automatic right to transfer to the academy school.

▷ If the predecessor school was selective or partially selective it can continue with these arrangements.

▷ Predecessor schools with religious characters maintain that character on conversion.

▷ Admissions – the trust must comply with the School Admissions Code and School Admissions Appeals Code.

▷ Charging – master funding agreement applies except in relation to former independent schools who have pupils from the non-European Economic area for whom it must charge the full cost of education.

More information

▶ Academy Governance Checklists:

    ▷ Funding agreement – master;

    ▷ Funding agreement – termination.

▶ Academy trusts – own funding agreements.

Funding agreement – termination

Introduction

All funding agreements contain termination clauses – although these operate slightly differently depending on whether the trust is a SAT or a MAT.

Dual termination clauses

Funding agreements allow for either party – secretary of state or academy trust – to terminate the funding agreement by giving seven years' financial notice. The funding agreement would terminate on 31 August in the relevant year.

However, there is a difference depending on whether the trust is a SAT or a MAT.

SATs run a single academy and, therefore, have one funding agreement. The seven-year termination clause appears in this document.

MATs have a master funding agreement and supplementary agreements for each academy in their trust. There is no seven-year clause in the master funding agreement for MATs. There is a seven-year clause in each supplementary funding agreement. This means that a MAT seeking to use this provision would need to give notice on each academy it wanted to terminate the agreement.

Other termination clauses

All funding agreements, whether for SATs, MAT master or MAT supplementary, contain other termination clauses. These would be activated by the DfE. There is a range of circumstances under which the DfE has the power to issue a termination notice. Funding agreements set out the detail, but they cover three broad headings: failure of governance or management; poor educational performance; and change of control.

Termination warning notices

Where the DfE is of the opinion that the trust is in breach of its funding agreement or any of the grounds set out in the termination clauses has been triggered it can issue a termination warning notice. If the academy trust cannot satisfy the DfE that it can remedy the situation then the trust can have its funding agreement terminated. In a SAT this will mean the trust will need to be wound up, the academy school will either be closed or transferred to another trust. In a MAT the DfE can terminate the funding agreement for a single academy within the trust but the MAT could still be left to operate other schools.

Checklist

▶ Academy trusts should be familiar with the termination clauses that apply to their academies.

▶ Termination clauses in supplementary agreements will be different to those in master funding agreements.

▶ Where a termination notice is issued trusts must comply with its requirements.

Procedure

▶ Termination warning letter – convene a meeting of the trustees to consider the warning notice.

▷ Agree a form of action.

▶ Chair of trustees to respond to warning notice.

▶ Act to wind-up the academy trust or transfer an academy to a different trust.

Notes

▶ Although the funding agreements allow for seven-year termination notice periods, this is unlikely ever to be used. A trust that no longer wants to operate is not going to wait seven years and will undoubtedly seek to merge or have its academies rebrokered. The DfE has a raft of other clauses at its disposal if it wishes to seek termination.

More information

▶ Academy Governance Checklists:

▷ Funding agreement – master;
▷ Funding agreement – supplementary.

▶ Academy trusts' own funding agreements.

▶ *Academy Governance Handbook*, Chapter 11.

General Annual Grant (GAG)

Introduction

The General Annual Grant (GAG) is the main source of revenue funding for academy trusts. It is calculated by the ESFA and paid annually at monthly intervals.

Academies are funded on the same basis as equivalent maintained schools. The GAG includes funding for day-to-day running costs and any other specific grants which are in operation at the time (e.g. currently academies with eligible pupils will also receive pupil premium funding and PE premium funding).

Academies with no predecessor schools may receive additional GAG during their start-up phase in recognition of the extra costs and lack of economies of scale. Some will have funding calculated based on estimated pupil numbers.

▷ Mainstream academies – the majority of revenue funding is calculated currently according to the formula the local authority in which the academy is situated uses to calculate funding for maintained schools. The formula factors used by LAs are set down in regulations.

▷ Special academies are funded on a per place basis (currently £10,000) plus top-up funding based on the needs of individual pupils. Top-up funding is calculated according to what the local authority would provide for the pupil in a maintained school.

▷ Alternative provision academies are also funded on a place and top-up basis.

▷ 16–19 academies are funded via a formula which takes pupil numbers as its starting point.

There is no specific grant funding for MATs – any central staff must be funded from the totality of the GAG funding.

Checklist

▷ The GAG is calculated for each academy within the trust.

▶ The ESFA notify academy trusts of the amount of GAG for each academy before the start of the financial year.

▶ The GAG is based on pupil characteristics collected via school census data.

▶ The GAG is revenue funding and is intended for spending on:

▷ teachers' salaries and related costs (including pension contributions, full- and part-time teaching staff and payments in respect of seconded teachers);

▷ non-teaching staff salaries and related costs (including pension contributions);

▷ employees' expenses;

▷ buying, maintaining, repairing and replacing teaching and learning materials and other educational equipment, including books and stationery;

▷ buying, maintaining, repairing and replacing other assets including ICT equipment and software, sports equipment and laboratory equipment and materials;

▷ examination fees;

▷ repairs, servicing and maintenance of buildings (including redecoration, heating, plumbing, lighting, etc.); maintenance of grounds (including boundary fences and walls); insurance; cleaning materials and contract cleaning; water and sewerage; fuel and light (including electricity and gas); rents; rates; purchase, maintenance, repairs and replacement of furniture and fittings;

▷ medical equipment and supplies;

▷ staff development (including in-service training);

▷ curriculum development;

▷ the costs of providing school meals for pupils (including the cost of providing free school lunches to pupils who are eligible to receive them), and any discretionary grants to pupils to meet the cost of pupil support, including support for pupils with SEN or disabilities;

▷ administration; and

▷ establishment expenses and other institutional costs.

▶ Academy trusts must only use the GAG for maintaining, carrying on, managing and developing the academies in accordance with their funding agreements, unless the Secretary of State has given specific consent for them to use the GAG for another charitable purpose.

▶ The GAG must not be used to fund adult education (except staff development), nursery education which is chargeable, children's centres or sports education or facilities not allowed for in the funding agreement.

▶ MATs may pool their GAG funding.

▶ Trustees must as part of their financial responsibilities and monitoring receive information about the level of GAG funding and make decisions about how it should be spent.

Notes

▶ The DfE is in the process of implementing a national funding formula (NFF). Once fully implemented this will fund every mainstream pupil with the same characteristics at the same level. As it requires primary legislation to introduce, the NFF has not yet been fully implemented and consequently funding levels vary across local authority areas. It is entirely possible for a MAT to have two very similar schools in different LA areas with significantly different funding.

▶ Trustees need to understand the overarching principles on which the GAG is calculated – i.e. pupil characteristics. Increasing or falling rolls will have an impact on funding. As funding is based on the October pupil census there will be a lag before any increase or decrease is felt. The CFO and senior executive leader need to be aware of these fluctuations and inform the trustees accordingly.

More information

▶ Academy Governance Checklists: Management accounts.

▶ DfE – academy funding pages – www.gov.uk/guidance/academies-funding-allocations

▶ *Academy Governance Handbook*, Chapter 11.

General Data Protection Regulations

Introduction

The General Data Protection Regulations (GDPR) came into force in May 2018. All academy trusts are subject to GDPR.

GDPR relates to the collection and use of personal data. Personal data is that which refers to an identifiable person who can be directly or indirectly identified by reference to an 'identifier'. There is a wide range of personal identifiers including name, photograph, audio/video recordings, identification number, location data or online identifier. Data can be held electronically or in paper filing systems. Some data is classed as 'special category data' because it is more sensitive – for example, information about an individual's: race, ethnic origin, politics, religion, trade union membership, genetics, biometrics (where used for identification purposes), health, sex life or sexual orientation.

Checklist

▶ Academy trusts must be compliant with GDPR.

GDPR data principles

▶ All personal data should be:

▷ processed in a fair, lawful and transparent manner;
▷ collected for specified, explicit and legitimate purposes and not further processed in a manner that is incompatible with those purposes;
▷ adequate, relevant and limited to what is necessary;
▷ accurate and where necessary kept up to date (inaccurate data should be erased or rectified without delay);
▷ kept in a form permitting identification for no longer than is necessary; and
▷ processed in a manner ensuring appropriate security of the personal data.

Academy trust's responsibilities

▶ The trustee board is ultimately accountable for the organisation's compliance with GDPR – arrangements for ensuring compliance can and should be delegated to staff.

▶ All academy trusts must have a data protection officer (DPO) – who is knowledgeable about GDPR and the trust's operations and policies and understands the rules on processing data:

  ▷ The DPO must be able to 'report directly to the board and conduct data protection impact assessments'.
  ▷ The DPO should be separate to those responsible for data processing decisions or the technology which protects it.

▶ Trustees need to ensure that their own communications and papers comply with GDPR.

▶ The trust's governance professional whether employed directly by the trust or otherwise must also comply with GDPR.

▶ All relevant policies must be GDPR compliant.

Notes

▶ GDPR was a significant undertaking for all organisations when it came into force. Trusts will hold significant amounts of personal data and sensitive personal data and need to ensure this is held securely and in accordance with the regulations.

▶ While trustees should not routinely be receiving information about individual members or staff or pupils this may occur in some contexts, e.g. if sitting on pay committees or exclusion panels. Person identifiers can include email addresses and trustees should consider how they communicate between each other and on what devices that information is held. Trustee boards are sometimes complacent about the data they receive as trustees but must consider whether the way it is received and held is GDPR compliant.

More information

▶ Academy Governance Checklists:

  ▷ Freedom of Information Act (FOI Act);
  ▷ Records management – retention and storage.

▶ *Academy Governance Handbook*, Chapter 9.

General meetings

Introduction

General meetings are meetings of the members of the academy trust.

The model articles allow for both an annual general meeting (this is a recommended but optional clause) and general meetings of members. All meeting except the AGM will be general meetings.

Any business which might be on the agenda for a general meeting can also be dealt with by written resolution – save a resolution to remove a director or auditor.

The model articles allow for either the trustee board to give notice of a general meeting, or the members to requisition a general meeting.

Checklist

▶ Trustee board convened – was the decision properly taken and recorded. Where there are insufficient trustees present in the UK a single trustee can call a meeting – this is unlikely to be the case in most academy trusts.

▶ Members requisitioned:

  ▷ Do the requisitioners meet the threshold for requisitioning a meeting? In the Companies Act the required threshold members holding at least 5% of the total voting rights.

  ▷ Has the notice of the requisition been sent to the company (i.e. the registered address) in hard copy of electronic format and has it been authenticated by the requisitioners?

  ▷ The request must state the general nature of business to be considered and may include the text of any resolution to be moved at the meeting.

Procedure

Calling the meeting

Trustee convened

▶ Convene a meeting of the trustees to consider the nature of any business to be put before members and if appropriate call a general meeting.

▷ A notice of the meeting should be issued giving 14 clear days' notice – unless 90% of members entitled to attend and vote have agreed to shorter notice.

▷ Ensure any prior consent is obtained – changes to the articles also require the Secretary of State's consent.

Member requisitioned

▷ Members must submit meeting request (electronically or hard copy) to the company's registered address – stating the general nature of business for discussion.

▷ Hold a trustees' meeting to consider the request.

▷ Trustees must call the general meeting within 21 days of receiving the valid request.

▷ The general meeting must take place within 28 days of the notice being issued – subject to any specific notice periods for resolutions.

▷ If the trustees fail to call a notice following a valid requisition the members have the power to do so themselves.

Prior to the meeting

▷ Check quorum requirements.

▷ Check chairing requirements – different versions of the model articles have different provisions.

▷ Ensure proxy forms have been checked and validated in advance of the meeting.

At the meeting

▷ The Quorum – which will be specified in the articles of association – sets out the number of people with voting rights who must be present at the start of the meeting and for business to proceed. Current model articles require two members to be present in person or by proxy for the meeting to be quorate.

▷ If it is not quorate the meeting cannot legitimately proceed.

▷ Check percentage of votes held by any local authority associated persons (LAAPs) – they may not exercise more than 19.9% of eligible votes at a general meeting.

▷ If the LAAP votes exceed the threshold other members' votes must be increased pro-rata to compensate.

▷ Trustees – all trustees are entitled to attend and speak at general meetings whether they are also members of the academy trust.

▷ Chair – model articles will specify who should chair – the current model provides for members to decide by ordinary resolution.

- Proxies – all members may appoint a person to attend in proxy or submit votes via proxy form.

- Voting is usually by a show of hands but can be poll if requested. A poll is usually a written ballot.

- Polls:

  - A poll can be requested by the chair or by at least two members attending and having the right to vote or a member who holds at least 10% of the voting rights.
  - A poll to decide the chair of the meeting or adjournment must take place immediately.
  - On other resolutions a poll must take place within 30 days of the request.

- Decisions:

  - Ordinary resolution – simple majority is required.
  - Special resolution – 75% majority of those voting required.

- Minutes should be prepared as soon as possible after the meeting.

Filing requirements

- This will depend on the notice and resolutions.

- Special resolutions will need to be filed with Companies House.

- Appointment of trustees will require notification to Companies House.

- Appointment of members or trustees will require notification to the ESFA via the GIAS website.

Notes

- The articles of association for the academy trust will set out the minimum number of members. The current model requires a minimum of three, but some early academy trusts have a single corporate member. More recent trusts are required by their articles to have a minimum of three members, but the DfE in the AFH states that it prefers trusts to have at least five. Numbers required to requisition a meeting, for a meeting to be quorate and votes needed to pass resolutions will be governed by how many members the trust has.

More information

- Academy Governance Checklists:

  - Annual general meeting;
  - Members – duties, liabilities and rights.

- *Academy Governance Handbook*, Chapter 6.

Get information about schools (GIAS)

Introduction

GIAS is the DfE's online register containing information about schools and colleges in England. It is publicly available.

Academy trusts can update the information via a secure login.

Checklist

▶ Ensure that appropriate staff within the trust have secure log-in details.

▶ All academy trusts are required to keep the details on GIAS up to date – trusts must confirm or update entries at least every 90 days. Reminders are sent to named contacts every 60 days.

Filing requirements

All academy trusts must submit: the names, date of appointment, method of appointment and where appropriate end of term of office for the following:

▶ members of academy trusts;

▶ chairs of academy trusts;

▶ trustees of academy trusts;

▶ chairs of academy committees – MATs;

▶ academy committee members – MATs;

▶ chief financial officers;

▶ accounting officers.

Notes

▶ Information on GIAS can be searched by the name of the trust, or the name of the academies within the trust. Once you have located the page for a specific trust or academy you will see a governance button, which will list those governing. Alternatively, if you know the name of the trustee/governor you want to search for you can use the find a governor tab on the main page.

More information

▶ DfE – GIAS website – https://get-information-schools.service.gov.uk

▶ *Academy Governance Handbook*, Chapter 9.

Good governance – principles of

Introduction

'Good governance in charities is not an optional extra, or a bureaucratic detail. Good governance is what underpins the delivery of a charity's purposes to the high standards expected by the public.'

(David Holdsworth, Deputy CEO, Charity Commission, August 2018)

In academy trusts the trustee board is the accountable body responsible for governance and for delivering its charitable purpose. Governance is separate and distinct from operational day-to-day management.

Checklist

Role of the trustee board in academy trusts

▶ To provide strategic leadership and direction.

▶ The DfE's *Governance Handbook* sets out three cores purposes of trustee boards:

▷ ensuring clarity of vision, ethos and strategic direction;
▷ holding executive leaders to account for the educational performance of the organisation and its pupils, and the effective and efficient performance management of staff; and
▷ overseeing the financial performance of the organisation and making sure its money is well spent.

▶ Governance plays a vital role in setting the culture of the organisation. Good governance is not simply about what is done, but how it is done.

▶ Academy trustee boards must govern in accordance with the statutory frameworks and guidance and in accordance with their governing documents. They should also have regard to guidance on good governance practice.

Nolan principles

▶ Academy trusts provide public services and are bound by the Nolan principles of public life: selflessness, integrity, objectivity, accountability, openness, honesty and leadership.

Governance codes

As charitable companies, academy trusts can look to two governance codes to provide examples of effective board practice:

▶ UK Corporate Governance Code – sets out its principles under five headings: board leadership and company purpose, division of responsibilities, composition, succession and evaluation, audit, risk and internal control and remuneration.

▶ Charity Code of Governance – works to seven not dissimilar headings: organisational purpose, leadership, integrity, decision- making, risk and control, board effectiveness, diversity and openness and accountability.

▶ Trusts can also consider the good governance standard for public life – which also has six core principles and supporting principles.

Role of members in academy trusts

▶ Members have a distinct but limited role as the guardians of the governance of the trust. The members' role is to hold the trustees to account for the effective governance of the trust.

▶ It is not the members' role to second-guess the board of trustees, or to become a 'secondary' board.

▶ Where there are serious issues with the governance of the trust the members can and should use their powers to remove and appoint trustees.

Procedure

▶ Boards should undertake regular self-evaluation and could assess how far they meet the principles of good governance set out in either one of the governance codes.

Filing requirements

None.

More information

▶ Academy Governance Checklists:

   ▷ Charity Governance Code;
   ▷ UK Corporate Governance Code.

▶ AFH 2018: www.gov.uk/government/publications/academies-financial-handbook

▶ Charity Governance Code for larger entities: www.charitygovernancecode.org/en/front-page

▶ DfE: www.gov.uk/government/publications/governance-handbook

   ▷ *Governance Handbook*.
   ▷ ·DfE Competency Framework for Governance.

▶ NGA – Academy trusts the role of members.

▶ Financial Reporting Council:

   ▷ UK Corporate Governance Code 2018: www.frc.org.uk/directors/corporate-governance-and-stewardship/uk-corporate-governance-code
   ▷ Guidance on board effectiveness 2018: www.frc.org.uk/getattachment/61232f60-a338-471b-ba5a-bfed25219147/2018-Guidance-on-Board-Effectiveness-FINAL.PDF

▶ Good Governance Standards in public services: www.jrf.org.uk/report/good-governance-standard-public-services

▶ Nolan principles: www.gov.uk/government/publications/the-7-principles-of-public-life/the-7-principles-of-public-life—2

▶ *Academy Governance Handbook*, Chapter 1.

Good Governance Standard for Public Services

Introduction

The Good Governance Standard for Public Services was developed by an Independent Commission and published in 2005.

The standard has six core principles, underpinned by supporting principles. It was developed to be used by any organisation delivering public services, including schools.

Checklist

The core supporting principles are:

▶ good governance means focusing on the organisation's purpose and on outcomes for citizens and service users;

▶ good governance means performing effectively in clearly defined functions and roles;

▶ good governance means promoting values for the whole organisation and demonstrating the values of good governance through behaviour;

▶ good governance means taking informed, transparent decisions and managing risk;

▶ good governance means developing the capacity and capability of the governing body to be effective; and

▶ good governance means engaging stakeholders and making accountability real.

Notes

▶ Academy trusts could use the standards as part of their regular self-evaluation, to identify areas of strength and areas which need further development.

More information

▶ Academy Governance Checklists:

    ▷ Charity Governance Code;

    ▷ UK Corporate Governance Code.

▶ Good Governance Standard for Public Services: www.jrf.org.uk/report/good-governance-standard-public-services

Governance Handbook

Introduction

The DfE publishes the *Governance Handbook*. The latest version was published in March 2019, with a further update promised for autumn 2019.

The handbook is for all state-funded schools: maintained, SATs and MATs.

It is available at www.gov.uk/government/publications/governance-handbook

Checklist

Purpose of the handbook

▶ Non-statutory guidance from the DfE, which sets out:

  ▷ the government's vision and priorities for effective governance;
  ▷ the core functions of governing boards; and
  ▷ the legal duties of governing boards.

▶ The chapter headings in the document are set out according to the DfE's six features of effective governance.

▶ The document is a mixture of guidance on good practice and legal requirements on governing boards.

▶ Where appropriate, it signposts to more detailed guidance and legislation.

▶ Academy trusts should read in conjunction with the AFH, which they must have regard to.

Who is the handbook for?

▶ Governance professionals should ensure they are familiar with the handbook.

▶ Trustees should be signposted to the handbook – it is not intended to be read in one chunk but is a useful reference document.

▶ Senior executive leaders should read the sections on governance practice.

More information

▶ AFH: www.gov.uk/government/publications/academies-financial-handbook

▶ DfE: www.gov.uk/government/publications/governance-handbook

  ▷ Clerking Competency Framework.
  ▷ Competency framework for governance.

▶ *Academy Governance Handbook*, Chapter 2.

Governance professional

Introduction

It is recognised across all sectors that for the board to be effective it needs high-quality support.

While academy trusts are required by their articles of association to appoint a clerk many trustee boards, particularly in MATs, have recognised that the size of the governance role means they need more professional support – akin to the Company Secretary role in corporate companies. This person, as well as providing advice and guidance to the trustee board, is likely to oversee governance across the academies within the trust.

Checklist

▶ The trustee board should have regard to the DfE's Clerking Competency Framework.

▶ The trustee board should appoint a suitably experienced and qualified governance professional.

Role of the governance professional

▶ Organise trustee board and committee meetings – providing advice on agendas.

▶ Ensure trustee board and committee meetings are properly constituted.

▶ Ensure the board follows correct procedures and complies with its governing documents and statutory duties.

▶ Provide independent advice and guidance to the board.

▶ Provide advice to the trustee board on good governance practice.

▶ Assist and advise on the induction, professional development, self-evaluation and recruitment of trustees.

▶ Be responsible for governance practice and process across the trust including at academy committee level.

Procedure

▷ The trustee board should be responsible for appointing the governance professional.

More information

▷ Academy Governance Checklists:

  ▷ Clerk to the board;
  ▷ Company secretary.

▷ DfE Clerking Competency Framework: www.gov.uk/government/publications/governance-handbook

▷ *Academy Governance Handbook*, Chapter 5.

Governance structures

Introduction

Academy trusts have a tiered formal governance structure which is determined by their legal status as charitable companies limited by guarantee.

The academy trust company is a legal entity, separate to its members and trustees. The 'company' can enter into contracts and own land.

The trustee board is 'responsible for the general control and management of the administration of the Academy trust'. The trustee board has considerable freedom to determine how to operate, what, if any committees it establishes and what powers and functions it chooses to delegate.

Checklist

Governance structure

SATs

▶ Members.

▶ Trustee board:

  ▷ trustee board committees – audit committee required, finance committee recommended – others at discretion of the board. Many trusts will have a standards or performance committee.

MATs

▶ Members.

▶ Trustee board:

  ▷ Trustee board committees – audit committee required, finance committee recommended, others at the discretion of the board. As with SATs many will have a standards/performance committee. In larger MATs this may be split into primary and secondary phase.
  ▷ Academy committees – the model articles allow for these to exist in every academy or across more than one academy. Academy

committees have no formal powers. It is for the trustee board to determine their role and function – e.g. whether they perform a monitoring role or have decision-making powers.

Requirements

▶ Check the requirements of the articles of association in relation to committees.

▶ Check the requirements of the AFH in relation to committees.

▶ Trustees boards must review the membership and terms of reference of any committees annually.

▶ The SoD should set out what powers and functions have been delegated.

▶ Trustee boards should review their effectiveness annually and consider and external review at least every three years.

Procedure

▶ Convene a meeting of the trustees – review and approve the SoD.

▶ Convene a meeting of the trustees – review the board effectiveness, including the working of any committees.

Filing requirements

None.

Notes

▶ No governance structure should be set in stone. They should be subject to regular review and refreshing. This will be particularly true in MATs where the governance structure will almost certainly need to change as the organisation becomes more mature or grows. What works when the MAT has fewer than six schools almost certainly won't when it grows to 10 or more.

More information

▶ Academy articles of association.

▶ Academy Governance Checklists: Financial scheme of delegation.

▶ *Academy Governance Handbook*, Chapter 3.

Governing documents

Introduction

The governing document is the legal document by which an organisation is administered.

For academy trusts their governing document are the articles of association.

The funding agreement is the formal contract between the DfE and academy trust and contains legal requirements in relation to the administration of the organisation, so should also be classed as a governing document.

Checklist

▶ The governance professional should have a thorough knowledge of the articles of association in order to provide advice.

▶ Trustees should act in accordance with the articles of association and funding agreement.

▶ Articles of association can only be amended with the approval of:

▷ the Secretary of State; and
▷ members of the academy trust.

More information

▶ Academy Governance Checklists:

▷ Articles of association – general;
▷ Funding agreement – master.

▶ Academy trust's own articles of association and funding agreement.

▶ *Academy governance Handbook*, Chapter 3.

Health and safety

Introduction

The trustee board in an academy trust is the direct of employer of staff and therefore has specific responsibilities under the Health and Safety at Work Act 1974. It also has responsibilities to pupils during the normal course of the school and in relation to any school trips.

There is also a general duty of care to other visitors to the site(s) of the academy trust.

Checklist

▶ The trustee board is accountable for health and safety – day-to-day responsibility can and should be delegated to the senior executive leader and other staff.

▶ The academy trust must have regard to legislation and any specific sector guidance.

  ▷ DfE health and safety responsibilities for schools.
  ▷ HSE guidance on health and safety in a school setting.
  ▷ DfE guidance on safe storage and disposal of hazardous substances.

▶ Academy trusts must appoint a competent person to take lead responsibility for health and safety.

▶ Academy trusts must have a health and safety policy which sets out roles and responsibilities and identifies key risks and how these will be managed.

  ▷ Must undertake regular H&S assessments – and must record any significant findings from it.

▶ Staff must receive health and safety training.

▶ Certain injuries to staff or pupils must be recorded and reported.

Procedures

▶ Senior executive leader should appoint an appropriately qualified member of staff to lead on health and safety.

▶ Health and safety risk assessment to be conducted.

▶ Health and safety policy should be submitted to the trustee board.

Asbestos

▶ Academy trusts have a duty under the Control of Asbestos Regulations 2012 (Regulations) to manage asbestos in their school buildings.

Filing requirements

▶ There are reporting requirements in relation to certain accident or injuries to pupils or staff.

▶ The DfE requires academy trusts to submit returns about asbestos on the school site.

More information

▶ DfE – Health and safety advice for schools: www.gov.uk/government/publications/health-and-safety-advice-for-schools/responsibilities-and-duties-for-schools

▶ HSE – guidance on managing health and safety in schools: www.hse.gov.uk/services/education/sensible-leadership/school-leaders.htm

▶ DfE – safe storage and disposal of hazardous substances: www.gov.uk/government/publications/storing-and-disposing-of-hazardous-chemicals-in-schools

▶ DfE – Managing asbestos in schools: www.gov.uk/government/publications/asbestos-management-in-schools—2

HM Treasury

Introduction

HM Treasury is the government department with overall responsibility for public finances. It also has responsibility for the tax system, including Value Added Tax (VAT).

Academy trusts must regard to some HM Treasury guidance and rules in relation to public expenditure.

Academy trusts are liable for VAT, but are also able to reclaim some VAT.

Checklist

▷ Trustee boards and accounting officers must act in accordance with HM Treasury's publication – Managing Public Money.

▷ Check whether VAT registration is required – threshold is £85,000/12 month period of VAT taxable turnover – i.e. everything sold which is not VAT exempt. Qualifying period is a rolling 12 months.

▷ Staff severance payments – have regard to Treasury rules.

Notes

▷ VAT is notoriously complicated and depending on the amounts involved this may be an area where trustees will need to seek specialist advice.

More information

▷ HM Treasury – Managing Public Money: www.gov.uk/government/publications/managing-public-money

▷ AFH 2018: www.gov.uk/government/publications/academies-financial-handbook

Insurance and risk protection arrangements

Introduction

The funding agreement requires that academy trusts have adequate insurance arrangements.

Academy trusts can either arrange their own commercial insurance or join the DfE's risk protection arrangements (RPA).

RPA

Originally, ATs had to ensure they were properly insured and the ESFA met the actual costs of the insurance premiums. This proved very expensive, and the DfE established the RPA as a means of reducing the costs. The RPA covers most of the major risks which academy trusts would need to insure against – although it makes clear not all risks are covered.

All academy trusts can opt into the RPA and can do so at any time. The cost of the RPA is currently £20 per pupil, per year or £20 per place, per year for special and alternative provision academies.

The DfE have said that for a one-off period from 1 September 2019 to 31 August 2020 the cost will be £18 per pupil, per year or £18 per place, per year for special and alternative provision academies. It has also said that the cost at £20 per pupil or less will be maintained until at least 31 August 2022.

Checklist

▷ Trustees must ensure that the trust is adequately insured.

▷ All employers are required to have employers' liability insurance.

▷ The AFH also suggests insurance to cover: buildings, contents, business continuity and public liability.

▷ Trusts should additionally consider trustee liability insurance, vehicle insurance, insurance to cover school trips, sickness absence management insurance, equipment and equipment inspection.

▷ If opting into RPA, consider whether additional insurance is needed for uncovered risks.

RPA

▶ AFH 2018 guidance is that trusts should consider opting into the RPA unless commercial insurance provides a better value.

▶ Consider whether the RPA offers better value than commercial insurance.

Procedures

▶ Trustees to consider whether commercial insurance or the RPA is better value.

▶ If appropriate, join the RPA scheme.

Notes

▶ The RPA has been very successful and roughly 65% of all academy trusts have now joined the scheme. As a result of the success of the RPA several commercial providers have revised the costs to academies downwards.

More information

▶ DfE RPA information: www.gov.uk/guidance/academies-risk-protection-arrangement-rpa

▶ *Academy Governance Handbook*, Chapter 7.

Keeping Children Safe in Education (KCSIE)

Introduction

The Education (Independent School Standards) Regulations 2014 place certain responsibilities on academy trusts in relation to safeguarding. The safeguarding duties cover both the welfare and safety of pupils and the requirement to make appropriate checks on staff and those governing in the trust. The standards also require the trust has regard to any guidance issue by the Secretary of State for Education. Keeping Children Safe in Education (September 2018) (KCSIE) is the DfE's statutory guidance in relation to safeguarding which all academy trusts must have regard to.

Checklist

▷ Academy trusts must have regard to the guidance in KCSIE.

▷ Academy trusts should appoint a member of the trustee board to take 'leadership responsibility' for safeguarding arrangements.

▷ Safeguarding is a collective responsibility and all trustees should understand their duties. Good practice would be for trustees to read parts 1–2 of KCSIE.

▷ Academy trust must have a designated safeguarding lead who should be a senior member of staff.

▷ All school staff should be provided with Part 1 of KCSIE at induction.

▷ Academy trusts must have effective policies in place to protect children's safety and welfare. This should include:

  ▷ an effective child protection policy which is updated annually and should be published on the website; and
  ▷ a staff behaviour/conduct policy which should include expectations in relation to: use of technology, staff/pupil relationship and use of social media.

▷ Mechanisms should be in place to ensure that safeguarding policies are understood and being followed.

▷ Academy trusts must ensure appropriate DBS checks are made on all staff, members, trustees and academy committee members.

Procedure

▶ Governance professional should remind trustees of the need for a lead board member for safeguarding.

▶ At a properly convened trustee meeting, trustees must determine the lead board member for safeguarding.

▶ Trustees should ensure there is a designated safeguarding lead who is a senior member of staff.

▶ Trustees should receive regular reports about safeguarding.

More information

▶ Academy Governance Checklists:

▷ Safeguarding;
▷ Working together to safeguard children and young people.

▶ DfE – KCSIE: www.gov.uk/government/publications/keeping-children-safe-in-education—2

▶ *Academy Governance Handbook*, Chapter 8.

Land and buildings collection tool

Introduction

The land and buildings collection tool is an online return developed by the DfE to provide information about academy buildings and land which must be included in the academies sector annual report and accounts (SARA).

Academy trusts with at least one open academy must complete the return.

Checklist

▶ Check the information contained in the land and buildings collection tool.

▶ Complete and submit in line with DfE deadlines.

Procedure

▶ This is an operational task – relevant members of staff should complete the return.

▶ Trustees should be informed it has been submitted.

Notes

▶ For existing academy trusts the 2018 tool was pre-populated with the previous year's information.

▶ The academies SARA is the means by which the DfE reports to Parliament and the National Audit Office about academy income and expenditure. The land and buildings collection tool was first introduced in 2017 in response to criticism (from the NAO and Parliament) that the DfE did not have accurate information about buildings and land held by ATs.

More information

▶ Academy Governance Checklists: Accounts – annual accounts return.

▶ DfE – land and buildings collection tool: www.gov.uk/government/publications/academies-land-and-buildings-collection-tool/land-and-buildings-collection-tool-summary-guidance-for-academies

Local authority associated persons

Introduction

The model articles of association make provisions to ensure that the trust avoids 'influenced company status'. This flows from one of the underlying principles of the academies movement – that they should be free from local authority (LA) control.

Local authority associated persons (LAAPs) are individuals directly connected with an LA. The articles place limits on how many members or trustees can be LAAPs.

Checklist

Definition of a LAAP

A person falls into the category of LAAP if:

▶ they are a member of a LA (elected councillor);

▶ they are an officer of the LA (direct employee);

▶ they are both an employee and either a director/trustee, manager, secretary or other similar officer of a company which is under the control of the LA, (this could be a teacher at a maintained school, a fire officer or a police officer); or

▶ at any time within the preceding four years they have been a member of the LA.

Definition of an LA

The following fall into the category of LA:

▶ county council;

▶ district council (including metropolitan boroughs, non-metropolitan districts/boroughs; and unitary authorities);

▶ London borough council;

▶ parish council; and

▶ community council.

Limits on LAAP participation

The model articles stipulate the following:

▶ LAAPs can never exercise more than 19.9% of eligible votes at a general meeting.

▷ Other members' votes will be increased pro-rata if this should occur.

▶ The number of LAAPs on the trustee board must be less than 20% of the total number of trustees.

▷ Trusts may not appoint a prospective trustee if this limit will be exceeded.

▶ If at a trustee meeting LAAP votes would account for more than 19.9% of the total, the votes of other trustees will be increased pro-rata.

▶ Prospective LAAP trustees may only be appointed if the LA with which they are associated has approved the appointment.

▶ If a member or trustee becomes a LAAP after appointment they will be deemed to have resigned with immediate effect.

▶ If at any time the number of member or trustees who are LAAPs amount to more than 20% of the members or trustees, then a sufficient number must resign to reduce the percentage. Those appointed or elected most recently will resign first.

▶ Members must inform the academy trust if at any point they think the academy trust has become subject to local authority influence.

▶ The LAAP provisions apply regardless of whether the LA to which a person is associated is different to the one the academy trust is situated in.

▶ The percentages apply even if the LAAPs are associated with different LAs.

Governance professional role

▶ Ensure LAAP status is included in eligibility criteria in recruitment packs.

▶ Advise the board on LAAP status and any action to be taken.

Procedure

▶ Member and trustee recruitment packs should include information about LAAP eligibility.

▶ LAAP status should be monitored to ensure overall limits are not exceeded.

▶ At general meetings governance professional to inform the chair if LAAP votes will exceed the valid limit and advise as to the remedy.

Notes

▶ Given the very wide definition of LAAPs and the fact that the skills of the people holding those roles are likely to be ones sought after by academy trusts, it may not be that difficult to reach the threshold. Governance professionals should keep clear records in order to ensure that the trust does not fall foul of the thresholds.

More information

▶ Academy Governance Checklists:

  ▷ Directors – appointment;
  ▷ Members – appointment;
  ▷ Trustees – appointment.

▶ *Academy Governance Handbook*, Chapter 4.

Local governing body

Introduction

In MATs the model articles allow for the trustee board to set up committees at academy level. In the model articles these are referred to as local governing bodies (LGBs).

LGBs are different to other committees of the trust as there is no requirement for them to contain any trustees. LGBs may variously be referred to as: academy committees, academy councils, advisory councils or a similar variation.

The detailed requirements relating to LGBs in this document are under the academy committee heading.

Checklist

▶ Check the articles of association for rules about the establishment of LGBs. Different versions of the articles have different wording.

▶ Check provisions in relation to composition.

▶ Where the trustee board has no parent trustees there must be provision for parental representation on the LGBs.

Filing requirements

▶ LGB members must be recorded onthe DfE's GIAS website.

More information

▶ Academy Governance Checklists:

  ▷ Academy committee – general
  ▷ Academy committees (composition, appointment, removal, resignation and term of office).

▶ *Academy Governance Handbook*, Chapter 4.

Management accounts

Introduction

Good-quality financial information is essential to enable trustees to carry out their responsibilities for ensuring that the academy trust's money is well-spent. Most organisations do this via management accounts.

These are usually produced monthly, and generally show income and expenditure against the budget set at the beginning of the year. A set of management accounts will show income received (GAG and self-generated). Expenditure will be reported against various cost-headings; e.g. staff, premises, energy, curriculum materials. The accounts should show the variations against predicted income and expenditure. Where the variation is significant it should be supplemented with narrative comment.

It is a matter for academy trusts to determine in what format the management accounts should be produced, but the AFH 2018 does contain some stipulations about their frequency and circulation.

Checklist

Management accounts should enable the board to:

▶ monitor financial performance;

▶ identify variation against budget;

▶ explain significant discrepancies;

▶ identify major areas of cost;

▶ monitor cashflow; and

▶ ensure the budget is being spent in line with strategic priorities.

AFH 2018 states that management accounts must:

▶ be sent to the chair of the trustee board each month;

▷ good practice would be to send also to the chair of the finance committee;

▶ be sent to all trustees at least six times a year; and

▷ be an agenda item at each trustee board meeting.

Notes

▷ The AFH requirements were new in the 2018 edition, but what is required is considered good governance practice in most sectors.

More information

▷ AFH 2018: www.gov.uk/government/publications/academies-financial-handbook

▷ ESFA – Academy trust management accounting: www.gov.uk/government/publications/academy-trust-financial-management-good-practice-guides/academy-trust-management-accounting

▷ *Academy Governance Handbook*, Chapter 12.

Members – appointment

Introduction

As charitable companies all academy trusts have members. How many members will depend on the individual articles of association. Some early academy trusts which were set up by sponsor organisations, have a single corporate member and others allow for all trustees to be members. However, the current version of the model articles requires a minimum of three members, but the AFH recommends at least five.

Checklist

▶ The signatories to the Memorandum will be the first members.

▶ Check the articles of association for the rules on member appointment.

▶ In some trusts the principal sponsor, or a foundation body, has the right to appoint some or all the other members.

▶ In many trusts the power to appoint new members will rest with the existing members.

　▷ Where this is the case, it is classed as a special resolution and requires 75% majority.
　▷ Members can be appointed at a general meeting or via written resolution.

▶ The AFH recommends that there should be at least five members – to increase diversity and to prevent situations where a special resolution would require unanimity because there are only three members.

▶ Current model articles prohibit employees from being appointed as members – this may not be the case in older trusts.

▶ Members must agree to their appointment in writing.

▶ New members must be placed on the register of members.

Procedure

▷ This will depend on who the power to appoint members is vested in.

▷ Where the members are responsible for appointing the procedure for calling a general meeting or for a written resolution should be followed.

▷ Once appointed members will need to be entered on the register of members.

▷ As a special resolution there will be filing requirements at Companies House.

Filing requirements

▷ New member must be entered on the trust's register of members.

▷ The ESAF must be notified via the GIAS website – within 14 days.

▷ Special resolutions need to be filed with Companies House.

Notes

▷ Although most articles of association stipulate that the legal minimum of members is three, the AFH 2018 recommends at least five. Academy trusts must have regard for the guidance in the AFH 2018 so should consider working towards its recommendation. Some trusts have struggled to pass resolutions as result of operating with only three members as special resolutions which require 75% majority require unanimity. Where relationship in trusts have become strained it can be difficult to pass necessary business. It is better to pre-empt such situations by increasing the number of members while all is on an even keel.

More information

▷ Academy Governance Checklists:

> Members – appointment;
> Members – duties, liabilities and rights;
> Members – cessation of office.

▷ *Academy Governance Handbook*, Chapter 4.

Members – cessation of office

Introduction

Members may cease office for a variety of reasons:

▶ they resign;

▶ they are removed from office by the person/body who appointed them;

▶ they are removed from office by the other members – this requires a special resolution;

▶ a member (which is a corporate entity) ceases to exist and is not replaced by a successor institution;

▶ a member (which is an individual) dies or becomes incapable by reason of illness or injury of managing and administering their own affairs; or

▶ a member becomes insolvent or makes any arrangement or composition with that member's creditors generally.

Checklist

▶ A member's resignation will only be valid if the minimum number of members stipulated in the articles remains in office.

▶ Where a member is proposed to be removed (by whatever means), if it would take the number of members below that stipulated in the articles it will be only be valid if accompanied by the appointment of replacement member.

▶ Members appointed by principal sponsors or foundation bodies can only be removed by those bodies – and not by special resolution.

▶ Corporate or foundation body members cannot be removed by the special resolution.

Procedure

▶ Resignation – the member should write to the academy trust (registered address) notifying it of their resignation.

▶ Removal by appointing person/body – send a written notice to the academy trust (registered address).

▶ Removal by other members – requires a special resolution (requires 75% majority) – this can be done via written resolution or calling a general meeting. (See separate sections on general meetings and written resolutions.)

Filing requirements

▶ Special resolution would need to be filed with Companies House.

▶ The ESFA would need to be notified via the GIAS website.

More information

▶ Academy Governance Checklists:

▷ General meetings;
▷ Members – appointment;
▷ Members – duties, liabilities and rights;
▷ Resolutions – written – members.

▶ Articles of association for the relevant academy trust.

▶ *Academy Governance Handbook*, Chapter 4.

Members – duties, liabilities and rights

Introduction

Academy trusts have members because of their status as charitable companies.

Checklist

Requirement to have members

▶ There is a requirement in the Companies Act for all companies to have members.

▶ Current model articles specify a minimum of three – individual trusts may have different requirements.

Legal responsibilities

▶ Members have no specific statutory duties.

▶ They are bound by the articles of association.

Members' rights

Members have rights derived from the CA2006. These are:

▶ to attend and vote at general meetings;

▶ to appoint a proxy to attend speak and vote on the member's behalf at general meetings;

▶ to vote on written resolutions of members;

▶ to be sent copies of the annual report and accounts;

▶ only members can approve changes to the articles of association;

▶ only members can approve a change to the name of the company;

▶ members have a right to remove any director, however appointed; and

▶ only members can remove the auditor before the end of the relevant period of office.

Rights deriving from the articles

▷ In the current model articles members have the right to appoint some trustees. The exact number will vary from trust to trust and in some cases will be the majority.

Liabilities

▷ On signing to become members they accept a limited liability of no more than £10 towards any debts should the academy trust be wound up while they are in office or within a year of them vacating office.

Procedures

▷ These will generally be governed by the CA2006 and are covered under the specific headings in this document.

Role of members in academy trusts

▷ Members have distinct but limited role as the guardians of the governance of the trust. The members' role is to hold the trustees to account for the effective governance of the trust.

▷ It is not the members' role to seek to second-guess the board of trustees, or to become a 'secondary' board.

▷ Where there are serious issues with the governance of the trust the members can and should use their powers to remove and appoint trustees.

Filing requirements

▷ Some decisions which rest with members will need to be filed at Companies House.

▷ Changes in members will be updated on the GIAS website.

More information

▷ Academy Governance Checklists:

> ▷ Annual general meetings;
> ▷ General meetings;
> ▷ Members – appointment;
> ▷ Members – cessation of office.

▷ AFH 2018.

▷ NGA – Role of members in academy trusts.

▷ *Academy Governance Handbook*, Chapter 4.

Memorandum of association

Introduction

Memorandums vary depending on the age of the company.

Pre-2009, companies had two documents a memorandum of association and articles of association. The company's objects were set out in the memorandum.

After 2009, objects were incorporated into the articles of association. The memorandum now just records the subscribers to the company.

To form a company, one or more persons must subscribe to a memorandum. In the case of academy trusts the subscribers are the first members.

Most academies were formed post-2009.

Filing requirements

▷ A copy of the memorandum must be filed with the other incorporation documents.

More information

▷ *Academy Governance Handbook*, Chapter 3.

Mergers

Introduction

Over time it has become more common for two or more SATs to consider merging to form a MAT or for two MATs to come together to form a new bigger MAT.

These are voluntary mergers as opposed to situations where the RSCs have used their powers to rebroker a school from one MAT into another.

Checklist

▶ In any merger at least one of the trusts will cease to exist.

▶ Both trusts should carry out a full due diligence exercise.

▶ Members must be informed as they will have to approve some part of the proposals.

▶ Staff, parents and where appropriate pupils should be consulted.

▶ Only the RSC can approve the merger and as a significant change to the academy trust will require the submission of a full business case. It is worth having an early conversation with the RSC's office to discuss the proposals.

▶ Trustee skills assessment should be done for the new trust – this will be a bigger enterprise and the trustee board might require a different skill set.

  ▷ The trustee board going forward should be comprised of those with the best skill set to govern the new trust successfully.

▶ If approved, the assets of one trust will need to be transferred to the new trust.

▶ The trust ceasing will need to be formally wound-up.

Procedure

▶ Convene trustee board to discuss and approve the formal proposal to merge.

▷ Convene members' meeting or propose written resolution to wind-up one of the trusts and/or change the name of the continuing trust.

▷ Submit formal business case to the RSC.

▷ File appropriate paperwork at Companies House.

Filing requirements

▷ Companies House of closure of one of the trusts.

▷ Possibly resolution for company name change.

▷ Continuing trust – notify Companies House of any change of trustees.

▷ ESFA – notification of any changes to members and trustees via the GIAS website.

More information

▷ *Academy Governance Handbook*, Chapter 3.

Minutes

Introduction

Minutes should be kept of all formal meetings: trustee meetings, trustee committee meetings, general meetings and meetings of any academy committees.

The model articles of association contain requirements as to minutes of trustee meetings and committee meetings.

Checklist

▶ The CA2006 requires that formal records of meetings of directors/ trustees and members are kept.

▶ Records of members' meetings must be kept at the registered address.

▶ Model articles stipulate that minutes of trustee meetings should be available for inspection:

▷ in a SAT at its academy; and
▷ in a MAT at every academy.

Access to records

▶ Articles of association stipulate that minutes should be available on request as soon as is practicable. Specifically, this also refers to the draft minutes once approved by the chair of the meeting and then the signed minutes.

▶ Academy trusts are subject to the FOI Act and must meet its requirements.

Procedure

▶ Minutes of a meeting should:

▷ be accurate;
▷ record where and when it took place;
▷ record who attended and in what capacity;
▷ confirm the quorum;

▷ while not verbatim, enable a reader to understand what was
   discussed; and
▷ record any decisions made.

▶ Minutes should be formally approved at the next meeting and signed
   by the chair (articles).

Storage

▶ Articles require that minutes are kept in a minute book – it is good
   practice to keep the agenda and supporting papers with the minutes.

Filing requirements

▶ No external requirements for minutes.

▶ General meetings – may be a requirement for resolution to be notified
   to Companies House.

Notes

▶ There is a balance to be struck between brevity and near verbatim
   reporting. The Charity Commission guidance – It's your decision –
   makes clear that where trustees have made a significant decision, the
   basis for that decision and the consideration trustees gave needs to be
   recorded. Without that record trustees cannot demonstrate that they
   have acted with due skill.

More information

▶ Academy Governance Checklists: Freedom of Information Act
   (FOI Act).

▶ Charity Commission Guidance – It's your decision: www.gov.uk/
   government/publications/its-your-decision-charity-trustees-and-
   decision-making

▶ ICSA Guidance Note Minute taking: www.icsa.org.uk/knowledge/
   minutetaking

Multi-academy trusts

Introduction

MATs are academy trusts which are responsible for more than one academy.

The vast majority of academies are now governed in MATs. There are over 1,000 MATs responsible for over 6,000 academies. They range from small MATs of two schools to the seven largest which have over 40 academies each.

Checklist

Legal entity

▶ A MAT is a single charitable company governed by one trustee board.

▶ It has a master funding agreement and supplementary agreements for each academy.

▶ The individual academies within the MAT have no separate identity.

▶ The AFH 2018 stipulates that there must be only one senior executive leader – usually with the title CEO.

Governance structure

▶ There are usually three layers of governance in a MAT: members, trustees and academy committee members.

▶ The articles allow (or may require) the trustee board to establish academy committees. Academy committees have no formal powers.

▶ It is for the trustee board to determine the governance arrangements across the MAT.

▶ The trustee board should have a vision and strategy for the MAT.

▶ All MATs must develop and publish an SoD setting out who in the organisation is entitled to make decisions and about what. It is critical to get this document right.

▷ Some MATs choose to run academy committees as advisory bodies with monitoring functions but no decision-making functions.

Funding

▷ Funding is calculated for each academy, but MATs have the power to pool GAG funding.

▷ MATs can choose whether to delegate financial decisions to academy delve or retain them centrally.

Size and growth

▷ There is no conclusive evidence of an optimal size for a MAT. Existing MATs are a diverse group, some primary only, some special only and some secondary only.

▷ MATs should plan carefully before expanding.

Notes

▷ MATs are very much the preferred option for the DfE and it is highly unlikely that most RSCs would approve any applications to establish a SAT.

National curriculum

Introduction

All maintained schools are required to teach the national curriculum (NC). The NC determines the subjects and standards which the government thinks children should be taught at particular ages.

Academy trusts are exempt from teaching the NC. Funding agreements require that the curriculum taught is broad and balanced.

Academy trusts are required to ensure that their pupils undergo the government statutory tests at Key Stage 1 and 2, and secondary age pupils can only take qualifications the Secretary of State has approved. In practice this means that very many academy trusts are teaching a curriculum which is very closely aligned to the NC.

More information

▷ DfE National Curriculum pages: www.gov.uk/national-curriculum

National Funding Formula

Introduction

The National Funding Formula (NFF) is the government's proposed mechanism for providing revenue funding to all types of mainstream state-funded schools.

Mainstream schools are currently funded according to the funding formula of the LA in which they are situated. This is the same for maintained and academy schools.

There has been a long campaign for fairer funding as under the existing system pupils with similar characteristics in different parts of the country are funded very differently.

The intention of the NFF is that one formula will apply to all state-funded schools in England. The DfE needs to make changes to primary legislation to fully implement the NFF and as yet that has not happened.

Currently the DfE uses the NFF formula to calculate funding to LAs, but LAs are then free to use their own formulae to calculate funding for schools.

NFF

The NFF is made of four overarching blocks containing a range of factors:

▶ Basic per pupil funding: basic per pupil funding and minimum pupil funding level.

▶ Additional needs funding: deprivation, low-prior attainment, English as an additional language and mobility (i.e. how many pupils enter and leave the school outside the usual time for admission).

▶ School-led funding: lump sum, sparsity, rates, PFI, exceptional premises and growth.

▶ Geographical funding: area cost adjustments (e.g. London weighting).

The DfE uses data collected through the school census and the LA to calculate a budget for each school. The aggregated sum then becomes the sum available for the LA to use its own formula to distribute.

Some LAs are moving of their own accord towards the NFF, but others are concerned about the turbulence the change may have on school budgets and are continuing to use their existing formula.

Checklist

▶ Academy trusts should be aware of the impact that the NFF will have on their funding and plan accordingly – although with no firm implementation date this is not straightforward.

Notes

▶ Funding for pupils with high needs is separate to the NFF. There is a campaign across the state-funded sector to increase the amount of funding to schools. Very many schools and academies are having serious difficulties in balancing their budgets.

More information

▶ Academy Governance Checklists: General Annual Grant (GAG).

▶ DfE – National Funding Formula: www.gov.uk/government/publications/national-funding-formula-for-schools-and-high-needs

National Governance Association

Introduction

The National Governance Association (NGA) is an independent charity representing and supporting governors, trustees and clerks in maintained schools and academies in England. The NGA's charitable objectives are to improve the wellbeing of children and young people by increasing the effectiveness of governing boards and promoting high standards.

The NGA is a membership organisation for all those governing, or with an interest in governance, in the state-funded sector in England. It provides advice, guidance, information, research and training. It sits on several DfE advisory groups and is recognised for its expertise in governance in the state-funded school sector.

The NGA is one of the five providers of the DfE's governance and clerking development programmes. The clerking development programme is accredited by ICSA.

More information

▷ NGA: www.nga.org.uk/Home.aspx

▷ Clerking development programme: www.nga.org.uk/ LeadingGovernance/Clerks.aspx

▷ Governance development programme: www.nga.org.uk/ LeadingGovernance.aspx

National leaders of governance

Introduction

National leaders of governance (NLGs) are designated by the DfE. They are experienced chairs of governors who have applied and met the DfE's criteria for designation.

The main role of NLGs is to support chairs of governors who are new to the role, or who are governing in a school in challenging circumstances. There is a range of scenarios which could fall within this remit. These are supporting someone chairing a school which has been:

▶ identified as needing significant improvement by the Department for Education, Ofsted, a teaching school, local authority or diocese; or

▶ where attainment is below the current minimum standards set by the government in transition to academy status or multi-academy trust.

Support may be face to face, via telephone or email, or a combination of all three.

Some NLGs will provide short-term support to governing bodies, for example, by joining an interim executive board or chairing a governing body in severe difficulties.

NLGs generally work with at least one teaching school.

NLGs are not paid for their support, but the school they govern at receives a small grant from which the NLG can claim expenses.

NCVO – Charity Ethical Principles

Introduction

The National Council for Voluntary Organisations (NCVO) is the national membership organisation for the voluntary sector.

On 18 January 2019 following a consultation it launched its Charity Ethical Principles, a framework to assist charities in meeting their charitable purpose ethically. The principles can be used by charities of all sizes and can help in making decisions and in developing relevant policies and procedures.

The framework is devised around four main principles:

- beneficiaries first;
- right to be safe;
- openness; and
- integrity.

Under each heading there is a definition of the principle and then examples of how to demonstrate that you are upholding them.

- Openness is defined as: charities should create a culture and space where donors and supporters, as well as the wider public, can see and understand how they work, how they deal with problems when they arise and how they spend their funds.

- To uphold the principle, you should operate a presumption of openness and transparency; subject to complying with existing legal and regulatory requirements, charities should be willing to share information about how they work, ensuring it is easily accessible.

Checklist

- Academy trusts should consider the principles and how to apply them to their own work.

More information

▶ NCVO Charity Ethical Principles: www.ncvo.org.uk/policy-and-research/ethics/ethical-principles?highlight=WyJldGhpY2FsIiwiZXRoa

Nolan principles and the framework for ethical leadership in education

Introduction

As deliverers of public services academy trusts are subject to the Nolan principles (otherwise known as the seven principles of public life).

Checklist

The principles should underpin everything that happens in the trust. All those in senior leadership positions, operational and volunteers should be familiar with them.

Nolan principles

▷ Selflessness – holders of public office should act solely in terms of the public interest.

▷ Integrity – holders of public office must avoid placing themselves under any obligation to people or organisations that might try inappropriately to influence them in their work. They should not act or take decisions in order to gain financial or other material benefits for themselves, their family, or their friends. They must declare and resolve any interests and relationships.

▷ Objectivity – holders of public office must act and take decisions impartially, fairly and on merit, using the best evidence and without discrimination or bias.

▷ Accountability – holders of public office are accountable to the public for their decisions and actions and must submit themselves to the scrutiny necessary to ensure this.

▷ Openness – holders of public office should act and take decisions in an open and transparent manner. Information should not be withheld from the public unless there are clear and lawful reasons for so doing.

▷ Honesty – holders of public office should be truthful.

▷ Leadership – holders of public office should exhibit these principles in their own behaviour. They should actively promote and robustly support the principles and be willing to challenge poor behaviour wherever it occurs.

Framework for ethical leadership in education

The Ethical Commission set up by the ASCL (Association of School and College Leaders) developed framework to build on the Nolan principles and develop something specifically for the school sector. It takes each of the principles and applies them to educational context.

▶ Selflessness – school and college leaders should act solely in the interest of children and young people.

▶ Integrity – school and college leaders must avoid placing themselves under any obligation to people or organisations that might try inappropriately to influence them in their work. Before acting and taking decisions, they must declare and resolve openly any perceived conflict of interest and relationships.

▶ Objectivity – school and college leaders must act and take decisions impartially and fairly, using the best evidence and without discrimination or bias. Leaders should be dispassionate, exercising judgement and analysis for the good of children and young people.

▶ Accountability – school and college leaders are accountable to the public for their decisions and actions and must submit themselves to the scrutiny necessary to ensure this.

▶ Openness – school and college leaders should expect to act and take decisions in an open and transparent manner. Information should not be withheld from scrutiny unless there are clear and lawful reasons for so doing.

▶ Honesty – school and college leaders should be truthful.

▶ Leadership – school and college leaders should exhibit these principles in their own behaviour. They should actively promote and robustly support the principles and be willing to challenge poor behaviour wherever it occurs. Leaders include both those who are paid to lead schools and colleges and those who volunteer to govern them.

The framework also identifies seven virtues which school leaders should demonstrate: trust, wisdom, kindness, justice, service, courage and optimism.

Notes

▶ The Commission continues to develop its work through an Ethics Forum and pathfinder projects.

More information

▶ Committee on Standards in Public life: www.gov.uk/government/publications/the-7-principles-of-public-life

▶ ASCL Ethical Commission: www.ascl.org.uk/policy/ascl-ethical-leadership-commission

▶ NCVO Charity Ethical Principles: www.ncvo.org.uk/policy-and-research/ethics/ethical-principles

Objects – charitable purposes

Introduction

All charities have charitable purposes (objects). The trustee board is charged with ensuring that the work of the charity is in pursuit of its objects and that charity funds are only spent towards meeting the objects.

Checklist

▶ The articles of association set out the charitable purposes of the academy trust.

▶ All academy trusts have the same core object of 'advancing for the public benefit education in the United Kingdom'.

▶ Individual objects will differ slightly depending on whether the trust is a SAT or MAT and whether it has special academies or academies with a religious character.

▶ The academy trust must always act within its objects.

Filing requirements

▶ Articles of association must be filed on incorporation at Companies House.

Ofqual

Introduction

The Office of Qualifications and Examinations Regulation (Ofqual) regulates qualifications, examinations and assessments in England.

Checklist

▶ Academy trust funding agreement state that they can only use GAG funding to support pupils taking qualifications approved by the Secretary of State. Ofqual is the body that approve qualifications on behalf of the Secretary of State.

Procedure

▶ Senior executive leaders will be responsible for approving qualifications taught and will need to assure trustees that they meet the requirements of the funding agreement and are appropriate for the young people.

Filing requirements

None.

More information

▶ Ofqual: www.gov.uk/government/organisations/ofqual

Ofsted

Introduction

The Office for Standards in Education, Children's Services and Skills (Ofsted) is the body designated by government and legislation to inspect maintained and independent schools, including academies.

Ofsted assesses schools against four headings and for overall effectiveness. It has just consulted on a new framework which is expected to come into force in September 2019. The basic structure of the inspection reporting will remain the same with four areas of focus, but it is proposed to change the headline figures and focus inspection more on what children and young people are learning, rather than on data and outcomes.

Except for schools judged to be outstanding and so exempt from routine inspection, schools are inspected according to a schedule.

Checklist

Ofsted judgements are important; depending on the outcome they can lead to trust being issued with a warning notice by the RSC which in a SAT could lead to the termination of the funding agreement.

Ofsted inspection judgements

▶ Outstanding – school will exempt from routine inspection.

▶ Good – school will be re-inspected approximately every four years, but this will be a 'short' inspection to confirm the school is still good.

▶ Requires improvement – schools will receive a full inspection usually within 30 months..

▶ Inadequate:

  ▷ Serious weaknesses – the school will be subject to Ofsted monitoring and will usually be re-inspected in 18 months.
  ▷ Special measures – the school will be subject to Ofsted monitoring and inspected when Ofsted deem it appropriate to do so but not later than 24 months.

▷ Maintained schools rated as inadequate will be automatically subject to an academy order. If a school in a trust is judged inadequate, then there will be a conversation with the RSC and a warning notice will be issued. If the trust doesn't subsequently demonstrate that it is improving the school, it may be rebrokered.

▷ When a school is converted, newly opened or rebrokered from another trust it will not be inspected until its third year of operation. This is in recognition of the fact that school improvement takes time.

Current areas which receive a graded judgement

▷ Effectiveness of leadership and management.

▷ Quality of teaching, learning and assessment.

▷ Personal development, behaviour and welfare.

▷ Outcomes for pupils.

Proposed Ofsted graded judgement categories

▷ Quality of education.

▷ Behaviour and attitudes.

▷ Personal development.

▷ Leadership and management.

Ofsted and MATs

There has been considerable debate since 2010 about Ofsted's role in assessing the effectiveness of MATs. Ofsted has no power to inspect MATs it can only inspect individual schools within them. Successive secretaries of state have been clear that they will not give Ofsted such a power.

Ofsted has carried out focused inspections of MATs. Where several schools in the MAT are due for inspection they are done at the same time. Ofsted also talks to other schools in the MAT and the senior executive lead. It then publishes a letter giving a broad-brush overall picture.

In December 2018 it announced a new strategy: the MAT summary evaluation.

This will be a two-stage process, some of which is voluntary on the part of the MAT. The two stages are as follows:

▷ Stage 1 – Ofsted will inspect a number of academies within the MAT usually over a two-term period (but could be much less if there are concerns) and publish their inspection reports (these will be academies due for inspection).

▷ Stage 2 – MAT summary evaluation will take place usually in the term following the academy inspections. Inspectors will meet and discuss with MAT leaders the inspection report and the overall quality of education in the MAT.

The second stage of the process is voluntary as Ofsted does not have the power to require MATs to take part.

What trustees need to know

▶ The most recent Ofsted judgements for school(s) in the trust.

▶ When the next Ofsted inspection is anticipated and the expected judgement.

▶ Ofsted assesses leadership and management which includes governance – in a SAT Ofsted will certainly speak to trustees, but they will also want to when a school is being inspected in a MAT – be prepared.

▶ Develop an understanding of the new framework before September.

Procedure

▶ Academy trusts should be prepared for an inspection visit; this includes trustees and academy committee members.

▶ It is useful to have a 'rota' of people who the operational staff will ring if Ofsted arrive – this will usually be the chair, but all those governing should be prepared. Ofsted do like to talk to more than one governor/trustee.

▶ If the inspection judgement is unexpectedly disappointing the trustees should seek to meet with the senior leadership team to understand why.

▶ The RSC will certainly write to the trust if the outcome is less than good.

Filing requirements

▶ Academy trusts are required to publish the most recent Ofsted report on the website of the individual academy.

More information

▶ Ofsted: www.gov.uk/government/organisations/ofsted

▶ *Academy Governance Handbook*, Chapter 2.

Parent teacher associations – and relation to academy trust

Introduction

Many schools have associated parent teacher associations (PTAs). While PTAs usually work closely with the individual schools, they are separate entities, often charities in their own right.

PTAs exist for the benefit of an individual school so in a MAT they will operate at academy level.

PTAs often raise substantial funds for the school.

Checklist

▷ The PTA will almost certainly be a separate entity with its own governance arrangements. Many PTAs are charities.

▷ A good relationship with the PTA is beneficial to both sides.

Procedure

▷ An established PTA will be responsible for following its own rules.

▷ Parentkind, the membership organisation for PTAs, has guidance on how to establish a PTA where one does not already exist.

Filing requirements

None for the academy trust.

Notes

Developing a good relationship with the PTA will have benefits for the academy. PTAs often raise considerable amounts of money and where good relationships have been fostered the trust and the PTA can jointly agree on areas where any funds will be most welcome and useful.

More information

▷ Parentkind: www.parentkind.org.uk

PE and sports premium

Introduction

The PE and sports premium is a grant paid by the DfE to all state-funded schools with primary age pupils. The aim of the grant is to increase fitness and increase participation in sport.

The grant is paid for academic years. In mainstream primaries this is for pupils in years 1–6. Some special schools have different age ranges and in these cases it is paid for children aged 5–10 as opposed to by year group. The PE premium is £1,000 per pupil for schools with fewer than 16 pupils and for all others a lump sum of £16,000 plus £10 per pupil.

Checklist

▶ The grant is paid to make additional sustainable improvements to PE and sports provision in schools. It cannot be used to pay for normal running costs relating to PE, e.g. teacher salaries. Academies are required to report on how the grant is used and spent. Specifically:

▷ how much funding was received;
▷ a full breakdown of how the funding has been or will be spent;
▷ the effect of the premium on pupils' PE and sport participation and attainment; and
▷ how the academy makes sure these improvements are sustainable.

Procedure

▶ This will depend on whether decisions about spending the premium have been delegated to academy level.

▶ Trustees will need to determine as part of the SoD what level of decisions on spending of the PE premium have been delegated.

Notes

▶ Regardless of whether spending decisions have been delegated to academy level, trustees should receive at least an annual report on the spending and impact of the PE premium.

More information

▷ DfE website – PE and Sports premium: www.gov.uk/guidance/pe-and-sport-premium-for-primary-schools

▷ Youth Sports Trust website: www.youthsporttrust.org/PE-sport-premium

Policies – other

Introduction

All organisations have policies and procedures to provide a framework for running the organisation.

Academy trusts are required to have some policies (see page 221) but there are others which are non-statutory but a matter of good practice. There are several HR policies which are not statutory, but it would be difficult to operate without. In some cases, these policies are statutory for maintained schools, but as academies have freedom to set their own terms and conditions are not compulsory.

Checklist

▷ In a MAT the trustee board needs to determine which policies will apply across all its schools and which (if any) it will leave to individual academies – some policies will require adaptation for different settings.

▷ Establish who will be responsible for policy development and approval – very few policies require board sign-off, so delegate.

▷ All policies should have a review date – ensure there is a schedule for review.

▷ The governance professional should maintain a list of policies and their review date.

Suggested policies

▷ Appraisal and performance management.

▷ Capability policy.

▷ Flexible working policy.

▷ Pay policy.

▷ Recruitment policy.

▷ Sickness absence management policy.

▶ Staff social media use policy.

▶ Trustees' code of conduct.

This list is not exhaustive.

Procedure

▶ Convene a trustees' meeting – trustees should formally delegate responsibility for policy/procedure development and where possible approval.

▶ The senior executive leader should delegate policy/procedure development to relevant staff.

▶ Some policies, e.g. HR-related policies, might be sourced from external professional advisers.

▶ It is good practice for the date of approval and date of review to be on the front of the policy.

Filing requirements

▶ No formal requirements for non-statutory policies.

▶ Policies relevant to staff should be easily accessible – preferably electronically.

More information

▶ Academy Governance Checklists: Policies – statutory.

Policies – statutory

Introduction

There are a range of policies/procedures which academy trusts are required to put in place. These requirements flow from a variety of documents, funding agreements, regulations and the AFH, to name a few.

It can be difficult to keep track of what is required and what is not.

Checklist

The DfE has a list of statutory policies academy trusts are required to have on their websites. It should be noted this has not been updated since 2014 and some of the information in relation to level of delegation was always inaccurate. For example, it still refers to a Home School Agreement but the requirement for schools to have this was abolished by the Deregulation Act 2015.

Required policies

The DfE lists the following policies:

▶ Accessibility Plan – Equality Act 2010.

▶ Admission arrangements – funding agreements. The trustee board will need to determine arrangements for each academy in the trust.

▶ Allegations of abuse against staff – procedure for dealing – KCSIE 2018.

▶ Charging and remissions – required by funding agreement.

▶ Child Protection procedures – KCSIE 2018.

▶ Complaints Procedure – The Education (Independent School Standards) Regulations 2014.

▶ Data Protection – Data Protection Act 1998.

▶ Equality Statement and Objectives, public sector equality duty – Equalities Act 2010.

▶ Financial scheme of delegation – AFH 2018.

▶ FOI Act publication scheme – Freedom of Information Act 2000.

▶ Health and safety – Health and Safety at Work Act 1974.

▶ Pupil premium strategy – funding agreements (depending on which version).

▶ School behaviour policy – The Education (Independent School Standards) Regulations 2014.

▶ Sex education policy – funding agreement (trusts should note that government policy in relation to sex education is changing).

▶ Scheme of delegation of governance functions – AFH 2018.

▶ Single Central Record – The Education (Independent School Standards) Regulations 2014.

▶ Special educational needs – Children and Families Act 2014.

▶ Supporting children with medical conditions – Children and Families Act 2014.

▶ Whistleblowing policy – AFH 2018.

Trusts should ensure they have all statutory policies in place and an appropriate review schedule.

Procedure

▶ Appropriate members of staff (possibly the governance professional) should ensure all statutory policies are in place.

▶ A review schedule should be in place and policies updated as necessary.

▶ Trust staff should be made aware of relevant policies.

Filing requirements

▶ In some cases, policies must be published on the trust or individual academy's website.

More information

▶ Academy Governance Checklists: Policies – other.

▶ DfE – Statutory policies for schools (treat with caution): www.gov.uk/government/publications/statutory-policies-for-schools

▶ *Academy Governance Handbook*, Chapter 8.

Principal

Introduction

Academy articles of association, the funding agreement and the AFH refer to the senior executive leader in a SAT as the principal. It is not a requirement that the trust uses this terminology and many leaders in SATs may still use the headteacher.

The title may also be used in MATs for those running academies within the MAT.

Checklist

▶ All academy trusts must have an AO which should be the senior executive leader – in a SAT that should be the principal/headteacher.

▶ The trustee board must appoint the AO in writing.

Procedure

▶ If the principal is also the accounting officer, then the trustee board should make that appointment in writing.

Filing requirements

▶ Requirement to notify the ESFA via the GIAS website.

More information

▶ Academy Governance Checklists: Accounting officer.

Principal regulator

Introduction

Exempt charities are regulated by a principal regulator rather than the Charity Commission. For academy trusts the principal regulator is the Secretary of State for Education. The DfE and ESFA fulfil this role on behalf of the Secretary of State.

Principal regulators have a duty under the Charities Act to do all they reasonably can to promote compliance by the trustees of the charities for which they are responsible with their legal obligations in exercising control and management of the administration of their charity.

Checklist

▷ Academy trusts are required to send their annual report and accounts to the ESFA within four months of the end of the financial year – i.e. by 31 December.

▷ Academy trusts are required to update the list of members, trustees, those on academy committee and the accounting officer on the GIAS website.

▷ The DfE and ESFA have the power to issue warning and termination notices to academy trusts.

Filing requirements

▷ Annual report and accounts must be submitted to the ESFA.

▷ Details of the accounting officer, members, trustee and those on academy committees must be placed on the GIAS website.

More information

▷ Academy Governance Checklists: Charity Commission for England and Wales.

▷ *Academy Governance Handbook*, Chapter 8.

Public accounts committee

Introduction

The Public Accounts Committee (PAC) is a select committee of the House of Commons.

This Committee scrutinises the value for money – the economy, efficiency and effectiveness – of public spending and generally holds the government and its civil servants to account for the delivery of public services.

It is the PAC which scrutinises the consolidated academy accounts when they are submitted by the DfE. It has also taken a considerable interest over several years in related party transactions. It was the PAC's report in 2018 which led to the DfE implementing the requirements in the AFH 2018 for transactions over £20,000 needing approval.

Occasionally the PAC will request the accounting officer or chair of an academy trust attend a committee session to give evidence.

Checklist

▷ The accounting officer should keep informed of any relevant PAC inquiries and report to the trustees as appropriate.

Procedure

None.

Filing requirements

None.

More information

▷ PAC website: www.parliament.uk/business/committees/committees-a-z/commons-select/public-accounts-committee/role

Publication of information

Introduction

Academy trusts are required by the AFH, funding agreement and regulations to publish various pieces of information and policies on their website. In MATs some information must be published on the website and the websites of its academies.

Checklist

▶ The academy trust must ensure that it complies with any requirement to documents or information within set timetables.

▶ Information trusts are required to publish:

▷ articles of association;
▷ annual report and accounts (by the end of January each year);
▷ funding agreement;
▷ governance structure – the structure and remit of the members, board of trustees, its committees and academy committees and the full names of the chair of each:
  – for each member who has served at any point over the past 12 months, their full names, date of appointment, date they stepped down (where applicable), and relevant business and pecuniary interests including governance roles in other educational institutions;
  – for each trustee and local governor who has served at any point over the past 12 months, their full names, date of appointment, term of office, date they stepped down (where applicable), who appointed them, and relevant business and pecuniary interests including governance roles in other educational institutions. If the accounting officer is not a trustee, their business and pecuniary interests must still be published;
  – for each trustee their attendance records at board and committee meetings over the last academic year;
  – for each academy committee members their attendance records at local governing body meetings over the last academic year; and
▷ scheme of delegation of governance functions.

▶ Each academy trust's funding agreement will specify what information it needs to publish. In a MAT some information must be published on the website of the individual academies within the MAT. The DfE has also published a list on its website.

Procedures

▶ The register of business interests must be updated annually and by individuals if something changes.

Filing requirements

▶ Publication of required information.

More information

▶ AFH 2018.

▶ DfE information academy trusts should publish: www.gov.uk/ guidance/what-academies-free-schools-and-colleges-should-publish-online

▶ Funding agreement.

Pupil premium

Introduction

The pupil premium grant was introduced as a measure to tackle the serious underperformance of disadvantaged children, particularly those eligible for free school meals. There has been a persistent gap between the achievement of these students and their peers for a considerable period.

Checklist

Pupil premium grant

▶ The grant is paid over the financial year 1 April – 31 March on a per-pupil basis to pupils who are in receipt of free school meals or have been at any point in the past six years.

> ▷ Primary pupils receive £1,320.
> ▷ Secondary pupils in Years 7–11 receive £935.

▶ Service children premium (£300):

> ▷ children with one parent in the armed services;
> ▷ children who have been registered as a 'service children' at any point since 2011;
> ▷ children of parents who have died while serving and are in receipt of a relevant service pension.

▶ There is also a premium for looked-after children:

> ▷ Children who have left local authority care as a result of adoption, a special guardianship order, a child arrangements order or have spent at least one day in care, attract funding of £2,300 order.
> ▷ The funding for pupils who attract £2,300 is managed by the virtual school head (VSH) in the relevant LA and the VSH is responsible for managing the funding. All LAs are required to appoint a VSH who does not occupy a school but has oversight of the progress and performance of all looked-after children, whichever schools they happen to attend, in the LA.

Reporting requirements

▷ Academy trusts need to check their funding agreement to check whether they are required to publish information or not. Depending on the date the trust signed the funding agreement, it may contain no reference to pupil premium.

▷ If a trust is required to publish information, then it must do so separately for each academy in the trust on that academy's website.

▷ The DfE recommends that all trusts publish even if there is no requirement.

Information to publish

▷ Details of your pupil premium strategy.

▷ How much pupil premium funding the received for the current academic year.

▷ Details of the main barriers to educational achievement that the disadvantaged children in your school face.

▷ How you will spend your pupil premium funding to overcome these barriers and the reasons for the approach you've chosen.

▷ How you will measure the effect of the pupil premium.

▷ The date of the next pupil premium strategy review.

For the previous academic year:

▷ how you spent your pupil premium funding; and

▷ what effect it had on the pupils.

Procedure

▷ The senior executive leader should submit a report to the trustee board with a proposed strategy and expenditure plan.

▷ Trustees can approve or request amendments.

▷ Trustees should monitor progress through the year.

▷ In MATs this will depend on whether the trustee board has delegated responsibility for pupil premium spending to the academy committee.

Filing requirements

▷ Publication of information on the website.

Notes

▷ Research last year by the NGA showed that there was a mismatch between identified barriers and spending priorities. Trustees should look closely at the proposed strategy to check that it is seeking to address the identified barriers.

More information

▷ NGA Research Spotlight on Disadvantage: the governing board's role in spending, monitoring and evaluating the pupil premium: www.nga.org.uk/Guidance/Research/Academic-year-2018-19/ Spotlight-on-disadvantage.aspx

▷ Education Endowment Foundation guidance for governing boards: https://educationendowmentfoundation.org.uk/tools/governors-guidance

Quorum

Introduction

A quorum is the minimum number of members or trustees that is needed at a meeting for business to proceed.

There are different quorums for members meetings, trustee board meeting and trust committee meetings.

Checklist

▶ Quorum – general meetings

▷ The current model articles state that quorum for a general meeting is two members present either in person, by proxy or properly nominated representative.

▷ All trusts should check their articles as different versions, particularly those where there are principal sponsors or foundation bodies as members, will be different.

▶ Quorum – trust committee meetings

▷ Under the current model articles, it is for the trustee board to decide the constitution and membership of any trustee committee. The trustee board should set a quorum when determining the terms of reference and constitution. The only restriction in the model articles is that a majority of the membership of the committee must be trustees and for any decision to be valid a majority of the committee present must be trustees.

▶ Quorum – trustees'/directors' meetings

▷ The current model articles set quorum for a meeting of the trustees as any three trustees, or where greater one-third of the trustees holding office, present at the meeting and entitled to vote. A quorum is higher where the trustees are voting on a proposal to remove the chair or a trustee. In these situations, the quorum is two-thirds rounded up to a whole number of the trustees in office, present at the meeting and entitled to vote.

▶ Quorum – academy committee meetings (MATs only)

▷ It is for trustees to determine the membership, terms of reference and proceedings of academy committees. The trustee board can, therefore, determine the quorum.

Procedure

▶ For all meetings check the required quorum in advance.

▶ At the meeting establish that the meeting is quorate before it proceeds.

▶ In the case of a general meeting proxies count to the quorum.

▶ Minute that the meeting was quorate.

Filing requirements

None.

More information

▶ *Academy Governance Handbook*, Chapter 3.

Records management – retention and storage

Introduction

Academy trusts are charitable companies and, therefore, records relating to the governance and management of the trust are covered by both company law and charity law and guidance.

This section covers the governance documents. Educational document and pupil records are covered by specific legislation.

Checklist

▷ Minutes of trustee meetings (including trustee committees) – for at least as long as the charity exists (Charities and meetings CC48).

▷ Minutes of AGMs and General Meetings – the Charity Commission is silent on retention, but as they may record important decisions about the charity, retain as long as charity exists.

▷ Agenda and papers for a meeting – the model articles of association say that these should be available for inspection along with the minutes. The minutes are the historical record so it may not be unreasonable to dispense with other papers to a shorter timescale. Trustees should take a view on what is reasonable.

▷ Annual report and accounts and financial documentation – six years requirement of AFH and HM Treasury.

Procedure

▷ The academy trust should develop a document retention policy which should record all types of data held, how long the trust intends to hold it and how it will dispose of it.

Filing requirements

None.

Notes

▷ The CA2006 states that minutes made after 2007 must be kept for at least 10 years, given that the Charity Commission guidance stipulates for as long as the charity exists (and potentially afterwards) it is better to err on the side of caution.

More information

▷ Charity Commission – CC48 Charities and meetings: www.gov.uk/government/publications/charities-and-meetings-cc48

Regional schools commissioners

Introduction

There are eight RSCs, one of whom also acts currently as the Interim National Schools Commissioner. Each RSC is responsible for a specific region.

Checklist

▷ The RSCs are responsible for approving new academies, changes to existing ones and monitoring the education performance of academy trusts and intervening in poorly performing trusts. They work closely with the ESFA.

▷ RSCs are advised and supported by headteacher boards (HTBs). The HTB members are non-executive although remunerated; the members' role is to provide advice, scrutiny and challenge to the RSC's decision-making. Decisions are ultimately for the RSCs to take, but they should be informed by the views of their HTB.

▷ All academy funding agreements set out the terms on which the Secretary of State for education can intervene in the academy trust on performance grounds. For MATs these grounds are set out in the supplementary funding agreement for each of the academies in the MAT. These powers are generally exercised by the RSCs on behalf of the secretary of state.

▷ Where the education performance of an academy is a cause for concern, the RSC has the power to issue a pre-warning or a warning notice. Where the RSC is not satisfied that a trust has the capacity to improve, it has the power to terminate the funding agreement. In MATs this is can be for the supplementary funding agreement for an individual academy, which will then be rebrokered to another trust, but in extremis could be the master funding agreement.

Procedure

▷ Where the academy trust is seeking to make a significant or minor change it must follow the procedures set out on the RSCs website.

More information

▶ Academy Governance Checklists: Department for Education (DfE).

▶ DfE – Schools Commissioner Group.

▶ *Academy Governance Handbook*, Chapter 1.

Register of directors

Introduction

Academy trusts are charitable companies and under the Companies Act must maintain a register of directors.

The register must be maintained at the registered office or the single alternative inspection address (SAIL).

Checklist

For each director, the following information must be held:

▶ name and any former name if change occurred less than 20 years ago;

▶ date of birth;

▶ business occupation (if any);

▶ service address; and

▶ country or state (or part of the United Kingdom) in which they are usually resident – e.g. England or Wales.

Register of directors' usual residential addresses

▶ The register of directors, which is available to the public, displays the director's 'service address' – usually the company's registered address. Companies must, however, keep a separate record of directors' residential addresses – this record is not available the public.

▶ The company must maintain a separate register with directors' usual residential addresses. If the address is the same as the service address or the residential address is the one given in the public register a note to that effect should be made.

More information

▶ Companies House Guidance: Guidance Company Registers.

Register of interests, members, trustees/directors, academy committees and staff

Introduction

The AFH requires that all academy trusts maintain a register of interests.

Checklist

The register must:

- capture relevant business and pecuniary interests of members, trustees, academy committee members and senior employees, including:

  - directorships, partnerships and employments with businesses;
  - trusteeships and governorships at other educational institutions and charities; and
  - for each interest: the name of the business; the nature of the business; the nature of the interest; and the date the interest began.

- Identify any relevant material interests from close family relationships between the academy trust's members, trustees or academy committee members. It must also identify relevant material interests arising from close family relationships between those individuals and employees:

  - A relative is defined as a close member of the family, or member of the same household, who may be expected to influence, or be influenced by, the person. This includes, but is not limited to, a child, parent, spouse or civil partner.
  - An individual or organisation carrying on business in partnership with the member, trustee or a relative of the member or trustee.
  - A company in which a member or the relative of a member (taken separately or together), and/or a trustee or the relative of a trustee (taken separately or together), holds more than 20% of the share capital or is entitled to exercise more than 20% of the voting power at any general meeting of that company.
  - An organisation which is controlled by a member or the relative of a member (acting separately or together), and/or a trustee or the relative of a trustee (acting separately or together). For

these purposes an organisation is controlled by an individual or organisation if that individual or organisation is able to secure that the affairs of the body are conducted in accordance with the individual's or organisation's wishes.

▷ Any individual or organisation given the right under the trust's articles of association to appoint a member or trustee of the academy trust; or anybody connected to such individual or organisation.

▷ Any individual or organisation recognised by the Secretary of State as a sponsor of the academy trust, or anybody connected to such individual or organisation.

▷ A body is connected to another individual or organisation if it is controlled by the individual or organisation, or controls the organisation, or is under common control with the individual or organisation. For these purposes, control means:

  – holding more than 20% of the share capital (or equivalent interest);

  – having the equivalent right to control management decisions of the body; or

  – having the right to appoint or remove a majority of the board or governing body.

▶ Trusts should consider whether any other interests should be registered.

▶ Boards of trustees should keep their register of interests up to date.

▶ Trusts must publish on their websites relevant business and pecuniary interests of members, trustees, academy committee members and accounting officers.

▶ Trusts have discretion over the publication of interests of any other individual named on the register.

Procedure

▶ All members, trustees, academy committee members, accounting officer and other senior employees should be asked to fill in the register of interests annually – this will usually be carried out by the governance professional.

▶ All those who have filled in a declaration should be reminded on a regular basis that any changes need to be recorded.

Notes

▶ There have been a number of instances in trusts which got into difficulties of close family members being employed either permanently or temporarily in the trust. Related party transactions have caused controversy and led to heightened scrutiny. It is important that all interests are recorded.

More information

▶ Academy Governance Checklists: Related party transactions.

▶ AFH 2018.

▶ The Charity Commission offers guidance in 'Manage a conflict of interest in your charity and CC29: Conflicts of interest: a guide for charity trustees'.

Register of members

Introduction

All companies are required to keep a register of members, either at the registered office address or SAIL address.

Checklist

▶ The following information needs to be included:

▷ name and address of each member;
▷ the date on which each member was registered as member; and
▷ the date a member ceased to be a member.

▶ As members can attend and vote at general meetings this record must be kept up to date.

Notes

▶ Records referring to former members may be deleted, but only after 10 years. It has not been unusual for academy trusts to be confused between members and trustees. It is critical this is sorted out and the correct names entered onto the register.

More information

▶ Companies House Guidance: Guidance Company Registers.

Register of persons with significant control

Introduction

All companies are required to keep a register of people with significant control (PSC Register). Its aim is to increase transparency. As charitable companies academy trusts must complete a PSC register.

Checklist

A PSC is a person who:

- holds directly or indirectly more than 25% of voting rights at general meeting – depending on how many members the trust has this could apply; or

- holds the right directly or indirectly to appoint or remove a majority of the board of trustees; or

- otherwise has the right to exercise or actually exercise significant influence or control and actually exercises or has the right to exercise significant influence or control over a trust or firm, which is not a legal person, which has significant control over the company.

The PSC register

- A trust must maintain a PSC register even if it has not identified a PSC.

- The PSC register cannot be blank – if the trust has not identified a PSC then the trust should use the most appropriate of the allowable statements.

Procedure

- Trusts should identify whether there are any PSCs.

- PSCs should be informed that they will be on the register.

- The register must be completed and updated as necessary.

- If a PSC is identified Companies House will also need to be notified.

Filing requirements

▶ Companies House if PSCs identified.

▶ Information will need to be verified annually as part of the confirmation statements.

Notes

While PSC registration was aimed at the corporate rather than charitable sector, all companies must make an assessment. Trusts where there are only three members would trigger registration.

More information

▶ Companies House Guidance – PSC requirements for companies and limited liability partnerships.

▶ *Academy Governance Handbook*, Chapter 1.

Register of secretaries

Introduction

All companies are required to keep a register of secretaries and this must be held at their registered office or the single alternative inspection location (SAIL).

A register must be kept if the trust has had a formally appointed secretary.

Checklist

▶ If a register is required it must record:

▷ name and former name if changed within 20 years;
▷ address – either residential or service; and
▷ dates of appointment and cessation of office.

Filing requirements

▶ Companies must notify Companies House if there is an appointed company secretary. Submit form AP03 or AP04 to Companies House.

More information

▶ Companies House Guidance: Guidance Company Registers.

Related party transactions

Introduction

Related party transactions are where the academy trust is contracting for goods or services with an individual who is classed as a 'related party'.

Checklist

▶ Related party transactions must be carried out at no more than cost where they amount to £2,500 in a single transaction or cumulatively in any one year.

▶ Related parties are defined in the AFH and are listed in the Register of Interest section of this publication.

▶ From 1 April 2019, academy trusts must:

  ▷ report all related party transaction to the ESFA before they take place using the online form;
  ▷ obtain prior approval for a related party transaction where the contract exceeds £20,000; this includes:
    – a contract of any value that would take the total value of contracts with the related party beyond £20,000 in the same financial year ending 31 August; or
    – a contract of any value if there have been contracts exceeding £20,000 individually or cumulatively with the related party in the same financial year ending 31 August.

Procedure

▶ Trusts should ensure that their register of interest is up to date.

▶ Build time into your processes to allow for the extra needed to seek approval from the ESFA for a related party transaction.

▶ Related party transactions will be reported separately in the annual report and accounts.

Notes

▶ Related party transactions are highly contentious. The rules in the AFH have been consistently tightened over time, largely as a result of external pressure, particularly from the PAC. While many people will at some point experience a conflict of interest, the financial element of related party transactions give rise to greater scrutiny. Trusts should ensure that all prospective members and trustees fill in declarator of interests as part of the requirement process – in order to enable potential conflicts to be caught early. It is generally better to avoid such conflicts than try and manage them, and where members/ trustees or their close family members wish to contract with the trust it may be better to suggest that they resign their position. Even with the 'at cost' provision the public perception is that those governing the trust are benefiting financially. The potential for reputation damage to the trust is quite high.

More information

▶ Academy Governance Checklists: Register of interests, members, trustees/directors, academy committees and staff.

▶ AFH 2018.

▶ Charity Commission Guidance – Conflicts of interest and It's your decision.

Religious character

Introduction

Some schools/academies are designated as having a religious character that may be attached to a denomination, e.g. Church of England, Methodist or Roman Catholic, or religion, e.g. Jewish. Where this is the case, there is a responsibility on the trustees to uphold the religious character of the school and it is likely to have a direct impact on what is taught in religious education lessons and on how the daily act of collective worship is delivered. If a school has a religious character before it becomes an academy that will be preserved after conversion.

In the same way, a trust cannot of its own volition attach a religious character to an academy. Any change in the religious character of a school would be classed as significant and require approval of the RSC.

Free schools which are established with a religious character can only reserve 50% of places for pupils of the faith. Schools with a religious character which convert keep their previous arrangements which can mean most of their places are reserved for pupils of the faith or denominations.

Checklist

▷ Where an academy trust takes on a school with a religious character the supplementary funding agreement will contain specific clauses. The trust will need to uphold the religious character of the school.

Notes

▷ There are some MATs which have some schools with and some without a religious character. The Secretary of State has signed a memorandum of understanding with the Church of England and Catholic Education Service which sets out key principles and ways of working for schools which are being converted.

More information

▶ DfE memorandum of understanding with the catholic education service: www.gov.uk/government/publications/church-schools-and-academies-memoranda-of-understanding

Reserves – including reserves policy

Introduction

It is prudent for any organisation to hold some reserves. Academies are in the unusual position in the charity sector that they have guaranteed annual funding and know before the start of the financial year how much that will be. It is also prudent, where possible, to set a little aside to cope with the unexpected.

Checklist

▶ Trustees are required to set out their reserves policy in the annual report and accounts.

▶ Where funds have been set aside the trustees need to explain why and what for.

▶ The AFH 2018 no longer sets a limit on how much GAG funding can be held over to another financial year.

▶ Financial planning should be an integral part of strategic planning – an unfinanced plan is unlikely to be realistic or achievable. It may be that some aspects of the plan require the trust to set aside some funding.

▶ Take advice on the levels of reserves which are prudent and achievable.

Procedure

▶ Trustees should discuss with their auditors the level of reserves considered prudent.

▶ The level of reserves must be discussed and agreed at a properly constituted trustees; meeting. This power can be delegated to the audit committee but may well benefit from a whole board discussion.

Notes

▷ In the current financial climate where so many schools are struggling it may not be possible for trusts to set aside very much in the way of surplus.

▷ While the AFH 2018 allows for pooled resources in MATs it also takes the view that this year's money is for this year's children and states that it will raise questions with any trust that has surplus for no good reason.

▷ Reserves have proved contentious in relation to MATs, especially where funding has been pooled. It is one of the most difficult areas to get past the 'my school' mentality.

Resolutions – members – types, majority, records and filing

Introduction

A members' resolution whether written or at a meeting is a formal decision of the charity.

Checklist

Companies – types of resolution and majorities

▶ As charitable companies legislation enables academy trust members to pass two types of resolution:

▷ Ordinary – which requires a simple majority to pass.
▷ Special – which requires a majority of not less than 75%.

▶ Special resolutions must be used for:

▷ changing the company name;
▷ changing the articles of association; and
▷ voluntary winding-up.

Notice period for meeting

▶ Model articles stipulate 14 clear days' notice for ordinary or special resolutions.

▶ Shorter notice can be given if 90% of the members entitled to attend and vote agree.

▶ If the resolution is to either remove a director or the auditors, then special notice is required. Special notice requires 28 clear days' notice.

Quorum

▶ This is two members either in person or by proxy.

▶ If a quorum is not reached within half an hour of the start of the meeting it will be adjourned to the same time at the same place the following week.

Voting

▶ Show of hands simple majority.

▶ Request for a poll – in effect a written ballot on the same basis as the show of hands as in most academy trusts each member has one vote.

Records

▶ Proper minutes of the meeting should be taken and circulated as soon as possible.

Filing requirements

▶ This will depend on the nature of the resolutions.

Notes

▶ Where academy trusts have only three members special resolutions will to all intents and purposes require a unanimous vote in favour.

More information

▶ Academy Governance Checklists:

▷ Annual general meetings;
▷ Resolutions – written – members.

▶ *Academy Governance Handbook*, Chapter 6.

Resolutions – written – members

Introduction

A written resolution approved by members is classed as a formal decision of members.

Checklist

▶ A written resolution requires the same majority of members to pass as a resolution at a general meeting. An ordinary resolution requires a simple majority to pass, special resolution not less than 75%.

▶ A written resolution is circulated to members – either as one document or more than one in similar form.

▶ The resolution will pass if a sufficient number of members sign the resolution and return within 28 days.

Records

▶ Signed resolutions should be kept with formal minutes of other meetings.

Filing requirements

▶ This will depend on the nature of the resolution.

More information

▶ Academy Governance Checklists:

  ▷ Annual general meeting;
  ▷ Resolutions – members – types, majority, records and filing.

▶ *Academy Governance Handbook*, Chapter 6.

Resolutions – written – trustees

Introduction

The model articles allow for the trustees to make a decision using a written resolution.

This can be used for decision by the full board of trustees or a trustee committee.

Checklist

▶ The resolution must be signed by all the trustees entitled to receive a notice of the relevant meeting, i.e. depending on whether this is the full board or a trustee committee.

▶ The resolution may be in the form of one document which is circulated and signed by all or several documents in the same form which are circulated and returned.

▶ Unlike written resolutions for members the articles do not specify a time period by which the resolution should be returned. If this provision is used it would be sensible to include one.

Procedure

▶ Written resolution to be circulated to all relevant trustees.

▶ It is good practice to include a date for return.

▶ Trustees return, having signed and dated.

Filing requirements

▶ Non-external.

▶ The returned form(s) should be kept with previous signed copies of the minutes.

Notes

▷ Decisions made at trustee meetings only require a simple majority
   to pass, whereas the written resolution requires unanimity. Such a
   procedure should be used sparingly – the benefit of a board is that
   they bring diverse views and a proposal at a meeting can be properly
   discussed.

More information

▷ *Academy Governance Handbook*, Chapter 6.

Risk (appetite, management, register)

Introduction

All organisations should have a risk management strategy and plan.

The AFH 2018 requires that the academy trust manages its risk. It says that the trust should have a risk register that the management of risk must include contingency and business continuity planning.

Checklist

Risk management

▶ Effective risk management encompasses a series of stages: identification, estimation, prioritisation, mitigation, monitoring and reporting.

Risk register

▶ A number of the steps are covered by a register.

▶ It can be useful to group risks together under appropriate headings, e.g.:

  ▷ educational;
  ▷ financial;
  ▷ governance;
  ▷ health and safety/premises;
  ▷ political;
  ▷ reputational;
  ▷ staffing.

▶ Under each heading the real or potential risks should be set down and ranked: what would be the impact if it did happen and what the likelihood is of it happening. You then need to include steps to mitigate against the risks.

Risk appetite

▶ It is important the trustee board and the senior executive agree on how much risk they are willing to take – if there is an undiscussed mismatch in views it may lead to discontentment and possibly conflict.

Business continuity

▶ This is highlighted in the AFH 2018. It may be that the chance of the risks which would affect business continuity are least likely to happen, but they would have the most impact. Trusts need to cater for fire, flood and at least as likely these days IT failure, malicious or otherwise.

Procedure

▶ The senior executive leader drafts the risk register.

▶ Convene a trustees' meeting where the risk register is discussed.

▶ The risk register is amended and refined.

▶ Senior executives monitor the risk on an operational basis.

▶ Trustees receive regular information, particularly if there is a change to the status of any risks.

Filing requirements

None.

More information

▶ *Academy Governance Handbook*, Chapter 7.

Safeguarding

Introduction

Safeguarding is an overarching term that covers all matters relating to pupil safety and welfare. It encompasses child protection arrangements and anti-bullying policies.

The Education (Independent School Standards) Regulations 2014 place certain responsibilities on academy trusts in relation to safeguarding. The safeguarding duties cover both the welfare and safety of pupils and the requirement to make appropriate checks on staff and those governing in the trust. The standards also require the trust has regard to any guidance issued by the Secretary of State for Education. There are two statutory guidance documents published by the government, *Working together to safeguard children*, which covers all those involved in safeguarding, and *Keeping Children Safe in Education* (September 2018) (KCSIE), which is the DfE's statutory guidance in relation to safeguarding which all academy trusts must have regard to.

Safeguarding and promoting the welfare of children is defined in KCSIE 2018 as:

▶ protecting children from maltreatment;

▶ preventing impairment of children's health or development;

▶ ensuring that children grow up in circumstances consistent with the provision of safe and effective care; and

▶ taking action to enable all children to have the best outcomes.

Checklist

▶ Academy trusts must have regard to the guidance in KCSIE.

▶ Academy trusts should appoint a member of the trustee board to take 'leadership responsibility' for safeguarding arrangements.

▶ Safeguarding is a collective responsibility and all trustees should understand their duties. Good practice would be for trustees to read parts 1–2 of KCSIE.

▷ Academy trust must have a designated safeguarding lead – who should be a senior member of staff.

▷ All school staff should be provided with Part 1 of KCSIE at induction.

▷ Academy trusts must have effective policies in place to protect children's safety and welfare. This should include:

  ▷ an effective child protection policy which is updated annually and should be published on the website; and
  ▷ a staff behaviour/conduct policy which should include expectations in relation to: use of technology, staff/pupil relationship and use of social media.

▷ Mechanisms should be in place to ensure that safeguarding policies are understood and being followed.

▷ Academy trusts must ensure appropriate DBS checks are made on all staff, members, trustees and academy committee members.

Procedure

▷ The governance professional should remind trustees of the need for a lead board member for safeguarding.

▷ At a properly convened trustee meeting, trustees must determine the lead board member for safeguarding.

▷ Trustees should ensure there is a designated safeguarding lead who is a senior member of staff.

▷ Trustees should receive regular reports about safeguarding.

More information

▷ Academy Governance Checklists:

  ▷ Safeguarding;
  ▷ Working together to safeguard children and young people.

▷ DfE – *Keeping Children Safe in Education*: www.gov.uk/government/publications/keeping-children-safe-in-education—2

▷ *Academy Governance Handbook*, Chapter 8.

Scheme of delegation (of governance functions)

Introduction

The SoD is one of the most important documents for trustees. While the SoD is undoubtedly critical in MATs every governing board needs one. Even in SATs the board must formally delegate powers to trustee committees and the senior executive leader. The SoD is the means to do this.

In both MATs and SATs the trustee board needs to decide which powers it will reserve for itself and which it will delegate.

Checklist

- Check the articles of association for any restrictions on what can be delegated – the current model articles provide a lot of freedom for trusts.

- The current model articles require that the terms of reference, constitution and membership of any committee must be reviewed annually.

- Delegated authority must be given in writing.

- The trustee board can revoke or amend delegation authority at any point.

- The trustee board may still exercise functions they have delegated.

- The AFH 2018 requires the SoD to be published on the trust's website.

- Decisions made without proper delegated authority may be invalid and subject to challenge.

- The SoD should be clear and unambiguous about what and to whom authority has been delegated – this is particularly essential in MATs.

- Decisions made by delegated authority must be reported back to the trustee board – this will usually be via the minutes of the relevant trustee/academy committee.

▶ The trustee board is also required to approve a written scheme of delegation of financial powers – this can form part of the overarching SoD or be a separate document.

▶ If you use a model SoD ensure you adapt it to your circumstances.

▶ The SoD is an important document – allow enough time on the board agenda to discuss it properly.

Procedure

▶ The senior executive leader and governance professional should work together to draft the SoD.

▶ The SoD must be approved at a properly convened and quorate trustee meeting.

▶ The chair along with the governance professional should ensure enough time is allowed on the agenda for the SoD to be properly discussed.

Notes

▶ The governance professional has an important role to play in offering advice on both what a good SoD looks like, but also about what it is good practice to delegate and what to reserve to the board.

▶ In SATs where the organisation is unlikely to have significantly changed it can be tempting just to roll-over the previous year's SoD, but it is important to consider whether it needs a more fundamental review.

▶ As MATs are more complex organisations it can take trustee boards a little while to decide what is the most effective governance structure, below board level, and what is the right level of delegation. Trustee boards must be honest, particularly with those at academy level, that the SoD is not set in stone and may change with time. This is also true for principals in academies within a MAT, who may have less decision-making power than a headteacher in a maintained school.

▶ Governance workload is a significant issue and there is an opportunity in reviewing the SoD to consider whether the tasks the trustee board is undertaking are necessary for the effective running of the organisation, or whether they could be delegated to operational staff.

More information

▶ Academy Governance Checklists:

▷ Delegation of authority;
▷ Financial scheme of delegation.

▶ DfE *Governance Handbook*.

▶ *Academy Governance Handbook*, Chapter 6.

School Admissions Code

Introduction

The *School Admissions Code* is statutory guidance published by the DfE which sets out the rules admission authorities must follow when determining admission arrangements, the timetable admission authorities must follow, who they must consult and what over-subscription criteria are allowable. The current code has been in operation since 2014.

There is a companion *School Admissions Appeal Code*.

Admission arrangements are the 'rules' under which children are admitted to schools, both the number of pupils the school has the capacity to admit and the criteria that will be used if more children than the school has places apply – these are known as over-subscription criteria.

All academy trusts are the admission authority for their academies. Academy trusts are required by their funding agreements to act in accordance with the *School Admissions Code* and the *School Admissions Appeal Code*.

The *School Admissions Code* is set out in three sections:

▷ Section 1: Determining Admission Arrangements – this sets out the rules admission authorities must follow in determining arrangements. It has guidance on acceptable over-subscription criteria and what may not be used. It provides the timetable for setting, consulting on and publishing admission arrangements.

▷ Section 2: Applications and Offers – this provides guidance on the co-ordinated admission scheme, how parents apply and the deadlines for making decisions on which children will be offered places.

▷ Section 3: Ensuring Fairness and Resolving Issues – this describes the way in which people can object to admission arrangements and make complaints to the Office of the Schools Adjudicator, the power of the Secretary of State to require an academy to admit a child.

Checklist

▶ The *Schools Admissions Code* is statutory guidance which must be followed.

▶ The academy trust must ensure that those in the trust with responsibility for determining admission arrangements understand the requirements of the code.

More information

▶ Academy Governance Checklists: Admissions – pupil admission arrangements.

School teachers' pay and conditions document

Introduction

The *School teachers' pay and conditions document* (STPCD) sets out the pay and conditions for teachers in maintained schools. All maintained schools must abide by its provisions. The document is revised annually.

Academy trusts are responsible for their own pay and conditions and are not required to follow the STPCD. The exception to this is in relation to staff who transferred from a predecessor maintained school – i.e. the staff worked at a maintained school which converted to academy status. All such staff are covered by the Transfer of Undertakings (Protection of Employment) Regulations, commonly referred to as TUPE. TUPE protects the terms and conditions of such staff to ensure they are not adversely affected by any such transfers. Where staff have transferred then they remain subject to the STPCD unless they subsequently agree to a change.

Many maintained schools which converted to SATs continued to use the STPCD as the basis for their pay and conditions. Many MATs also use the STPCD as a framework for their pay and conditions, particularly for those working at academy level.

The document is set out in two sections. The first section is purely background and introduction. Section 2 is in seven parts and provides the detail of pay ranges, allowances and contractual obligations.

▷ Part 1 – Pay general – this starts by giving the details of the annual pay award (if there has been one). It also sets out legal entitlements, timescales for determining awards and the requirement for pay authorities to have pay policies and appeal mechanisms.

▷ Part 2 – Leadership group pay – sets out how the leadership group pay ranges and how pay for headteachers and deputies should be determined.

▷ Part 3 – Other teachers' pay ranges – there are four ranges for teachers: main, upper, leading practitioner and unqualified. It sets out the pay ranges, how pay should be determined and the overarching rules about applying to be on the upper pay range.

▶ Part 4 – Allowances and other payments for classroom teachers – sets out the range of allowances which are allowable and the grounds on which these can be paid.

▶ Part 5 – Safeguarding – in this context is about salary protection, i.e. when a change would result in teacher's salary being reduced it can be protected for a three-year period.

▶ Part 6 – Supplementary – in effect miscellaneous issues which don't fit elsewhere.

▶ Part 7 – Contractual Framework for teachers – this is an important section as it sets out the contractual obligations and rights of headteachers and teachers.

Checklist

▶ Academy trust must be clear about which staff are covered by TUPE and have rights associated with the STPCD. As the vast majority of academies were previously maintained schools this is likely to apply to many teaching staff.

▶ Trustee board will need to determine whether they will adopt the STPCD in full or part in relation to the academy trust's pay and conditions document.

Procedure

▶ Trustees must determine the pay and overarching conditions of employment – policies should be approved at a properly constituted meeting of the trustee board.

Notes

▶ Trustees can determine to adopt the provisions of the STPCD in full, part or not at all. Staff with TUPE protections will still be covered by the STPCD.

▶ While the STPCD does have some provisions for a senior executive leader responsible for more than one school, it is not extensive and the larger the MAT the less relevance it will have. Executive pay has been a contentious issue and the AFH contains provisions which trusts must follow.

▶ Several researcher groups have found that when looking at reasons for schools converting, pay and conditions freedom was not high on the list. Trusts need to weigh the benefits and disadvantages of moving from an established framework and developing their own terms and conditions.

More information

▷ STPCD.

▷ AFH 2018.

▷ DfE *Governance Handbook*.

▷ *Academy Governance Handbook*, Chapter 10.

Senior executive leader

Introduction

The senior executive leader is the term adopted by the DfE and ESFA to refer to the most senior member of staff in an academy trust. Trusts use different terms for this post, and it was necessary to find a term that applied in SATs or MATs.

The AFH requires that all trusts have a senior executive leader. This person is usually also the accounting officer.

The senior executive leader may be known as the chief executive officer, executive headteacher, executive principal, headteacher or principal. The title in use is a matter for the trustee board.

Checklist

▷ Ensure that relevant people, staff, trustees and those at academy level understand what is meant by senior executive leader in DfE and ESFA guidance.

▷ Ensure the trust has followed the AFH 2018 and there is a senior executive leader.

Notes

▷ In some early MATs an approach was taken which saw the 'senior' role being shared out – where the headteachers of the academies in the MAT would each 'take a turn'. This is now prohibited by the AFH and all trusts must have one senior executive leader and this role must not 'rotate'.

▷ All organisations need clarity of role and leadership – the person who is ultimately accountable to the board for the performance – the final port of call as it were. It is of course possible for this to be a job-share position.

More information

▶ Academy Governance Checklists:

 ▷ Chief executive officer;
 ▷ Executive headteacher.

▶ AFH 2018.

▶ *Academy Governance Handbook*, Chapters 12 and 4.

Single academy trusts

Introduction

SATs are trusts with responsibility for a single academy. To all intents and purpose the trust is indistinguishable from the academy. All SATs are charitable companies.

A SAT has one funding agreement (as opposed to a MAT which has a master and supplementaries). It has its own articles of association.

When the Academies Act 2010 was passed, most schools which converted did so as SATs.

The DfE's preference has now changed and it sees MATs as offering better long-term prospects for educational performance and financial stability.

Many schools which originally converted to SATs have since become MATs.

Checklist

▶ A school wishing to convert to a SAT must follow the procedure on the DfE's website and will need approval by the RSC.

▶ Groups wishing to establish a free school as a SAT should also follow DfE guidance.

Procedure

▶ The maintained school governing board would need to decide to convert to academy status.

▶ Apply for an academy order following the procedure on the DfE's website.

▶ Free school proposers would need to show they have the capacity to run a school, but also that there is a genuine call for one in their area. They should look at the advice on both the DfE and New Schools Network website.

Notes

▶ Legally it is possible for SATs to be formed. However, given DfE's policy priorities the reality is that any application is unlikely to be approved.

▶ Although there are more SATs than MATs – as at September 2018, 59% of all academy trusts were SATs – the vast majority of academies are in MATs. From the same statistics there were 1,686 SATs but 6,491 academies in MATs.

▶ There also a number of 'empty' MATs which have not yet taken on additional schools.

Special educational needs and disabilities (SEND)

Introduction

A child or young person has special education needs and disabilities (SEND) if they have a learning difficulty or disability that calls for special educational provision to be made for him or her. A child of compulsory school age or a young person has a learning difficulty or disability if they:

▶ have significantly greater difficulty in learning than the majority of others of the same age; or

▶ have a disability that prevents or hinders them from making use of facilities of a kind generally provided for others of the same age in mainstream schools or mainstream post-16 institutions.

Section 66 of the Children and Families Act 2014 places a duty on the academy trust to use 'its best endeavours' to make sure that the SEND of any pupil is met. All academy trusts must have regard to the Special educational needs and disability code of practice: 0 to 25 years statutory guidance document which sets out what provision schools must make for pupils with SEND.

Most children with SEND are identified by their school setting and their needs are met within that individual setting. Some children have a higher level of need in which case it may be appropriate to apply for a formal assessment of their needs. The formal assessment is carried out by the LA at the request of either the parents or schools. A formal assessment may lead to a child being provided with an Education Health and Care Plan (EHCP). EHCPs specify the special educational provision required to meet each of the child or young person's special educational needs. EHCPs should be focused on education and training, and health and care outcomes that will enable children and young people to progress in their learning and, as they get older, to be well prepared for adulthood.

The EHCP his is a statutory document and any academy trust with pupils with EHCPs must follow its provisions. Given the greater level of need of children with EHCPs the local authority may also provide additional funding.

In special academies all the pupils generally have EHCPs.

Checklist

▶ Trustee boards must understand their duties in relation to pupils with SEND – these are set out in the *SEND Code of practice*.

▶ Trustee boards should receive regular reports on the progress of pupils with SEND.

▶ All academies must appoint a Special Needs Co-ordinator (SENCO), who takes responsibility for ensuring children with SEND are identified, assessed and have their needs met. MATs can appoint a SENCO across more than one academy, but they must be able to fulfil their responsibilities to the pupils.

▶ An EHCP names the educational institution that the child is to attend. Academies cannot refuse to admit a child if they are named on the EHCP. Where the child is not a pupil the academy will be consulted and could at that stage make representations if they have genuine concerns about the ability of the academy to meet the assessed needs of the pupil. The presumption is that all pupils will be educated in mainstream schools and parents have the right to express a preference as to which school that is.

▶ Academy trusts must publish certain information on the website of individual academies. The information should be updated annually and any changes occurring during the year should be updated as soon as possible. The information to be published is set out in the Special Educational Needs and Disabilities Regulations 2014.

▶ Depending on when your funding agreement was signed it may contain other specific requirements in relation to publication of information.

Procedure

▶ Appointment of SENCO: each mainstream academy must have a SENCO – the trustee board can delegate the appointment. The SoD needs to indicate who is responsible for which staffing appointments.

Standards testing agency

Introduction

The Standards and Testing Agency (STA) is an executive agency of the DfE. It has responsibility for setting the statutory assessment tests for early years, Key Stage 1 and Key Stage 2 pupils. It is also responsible for the professional skills tests for trainee tests.

Most interaction between academy trusts and the STA will be through professional staff.

Academy trusts are required by their funding agreements to administer statutory tests. The outcomes of Key Stage 2 tests are published on the DfE's Compare School Performance website.

The STA has a statutory responsibility to investigate any concern about the accuracy of Key Stage 1 or 2 tests. It has the power to annul some or of a school's results where the concerns are validated.

More information

▷ STA website: www.gov.uk/government/organisations/standards-and-testing-agency

Studio schools

Introduction

Studio schools are a specific type of academy. They are secondary schools catering for pupils aged 14–19. They are small for secondary schools (usually with around 300 pupils). The schools teach mainstream qualifications but do so through project-based learning.

Students work with local employers and a personal coach, and follow a curriculum designed to give them the skills and qualifications they need in work, or to take up further education.

Legally, studio schools will be run by an academy trust. They may be SATs or in a MAT.

Procedure

▶ There is a specific application process for setting up a studio school. The DfE website contains guidance and the application form.

Notes

▶ Studio schools have struggled to establish themselves and a number have closed. 300 capacity is small for secondary schools in any case, but often studio schools have struggled to recruit to their capacity. Undoubtedly part of the problem is that generally they are seeking to recruit pupils at an age which is not a common changing point. Most secondary schools are 11–16 or 11–18 so pupils are leaving part-way through the school. Schools have been 'reluctant' to promote studio schools or UTCs knowing that it will affect the number on roll at their schools and consequently have knock-on effects on the budget. It can also be difficult to persuade pupils to move to a new school, leaving friends and familiar surroundings.

▶ It may be that studio schools will have better success within a MAT setting with the potential for pooling resources.

Teachers' pension scheme

Introduction

The teachers' pension scheme (TPS) is the statutory pension scheme for teachers in state-funded schools.

All state-funded schools are required to pay into the TPS for any teachers in their employ.

Teachers in state-funded schools have an automatic right to be enrolled in the TPS.

Checklist

▶ Academy trusts are required by their funding agreement to provide access to the TPS for all teaching staff and meet any requirements of the scheme.

▶ Reports on pensions contributions (and liabilities for non-teaching staff) should form part of the regular suite of finance papers for the trustee board.

▶ The employer's contribution (i.e. what the academy trust has to pay) is currently 16.48% of salary but as result of the cyclical re-evaluation is likely to increase to around 24% from September 2020.

▶ Academy trusts need to ensure that the cost of pensions contributions including the scheduled increase are included in budget and expenditure forecast.

Procedure

▶ Teaching staff should be automatically enrolled in the TPS – this is an operational matter.

▶ The academy trust's employer's contributions should be dealt with by operational staff.

▶ The trustee finance committee should receive regular information about pension contributions and liabilities.

Notes

▶ The DfE consulted on grant payment to cover the costs of the increased pension contributions during early 2019. Academy trusts should receive additional funding to cover the costs of the increase. As with any grant funding, the mechanism used will mean that it won't be like-for-like cover – trusts will need to budget for this.

More information

▶ Teachers' pension scheme website: www.teacherspensions.co.uk/employers/employer-hub.aspx

Teaching schools

Introduction

Teaching schools can be any type of state-funded school. They are effective schools who work with other schools to provide high-quality training, development and support to new and experienced school staff.

Schools must apply through a formal process to the DfE to be designated as a teaching school. The designation is given to an individual institution rather than an organisation. Many MATs have one or more teaching schools within them – but it is the academy to which the designation applies.

Checklist

▶ The current expected role of teaching schools is described on the DfE website as to:

▷ co-ordinate and provide high-quality school-led initial teacher training (ITT);
▷ provide high-quality school-to-school support to spread excellent practice, particularly to schools that need it most; and
▷ provide evidence-based professional and leadership development for teachers and leaders across their network.

Eligibility

▷ There is not an open round for applications at present. The criteria have been tweaked slightly over the years rather than substantially changed. To be eligible to apply both the school and headteacher must be a least good, In the case of the school the last Ofsted must be good and in the headteacher's case they must have had at least three years' experience and is named on an Ofsted report as a headteacher of a good school. Other criteria generally centre around demonstrating that the school and head have a good track record in school to school support.

Trustee board's role

▷ Trustee boards should be aware of any existing teaching school obligations.

▷ Trustee boards will need to sign off support any new applications.

Procedures

▶ The trustee board must sign teaching school application to demonstrate a commitment to allow staff to provide external support.

Notes

▶ Many academy trusts will be teaching schools or have one within their MAT.

More information

▶ DfE website – teaching schools: www.gov.uk/government/collections/teaching-schools-and-system-leadership-how-you-can-get-involved

Trading subsidiary

Introduction

Trading subsidiaries are generally set up by charities to undertake training enterprises which the main charity could not do because they would either be considered 'too risky' or do not fall within the charitable purposes. For example, many well-known charities have trading subsidiaries with shops which sell cards, household items or clothes – but their charitable purposes relate to animal or child welfare.

Trading subsidiaries funnel money back into the main charity usually via gift aid which has tax advantages.

Checklist

▶ Trustees need to consider carefully the risks involved in any trading.

▶ Setting up a separate company is time consuming and would still need to be managed.

▶ The trustee board must seek professional advice if they are thinking of setting up a trading subsidiary.

Procedure

▶ Companies House procedures need to be followed if the trust wishes to set up a trading subsidiary, which would be a separate company.

▶ The trustee board first needs to make a formal decision to set up a trading subsidiary.

▶ The first step would be paper to the board of trustees to consider the options – this must involve professional advice.

Notes

▷ Academy trusts can set up trading subsidiaries, but trustees would need to ask whether this was a practical or sensible option. Any trading the academy trust undertakes, e.g. selling improvement services to other educational institutions, is likely to fall with its charitable objects, meaning the trust can trade without a separate company. Having a separate company does involve extra work and scrutiny by the trustees. Professional advice at an early stage is essential.

Trustee committees

Introduction

Very many boards, charitable or otherwise establish committees in order to enable more detailed scrutiny of aspects of the board's work. In the school sector these have traditionally been focused on finance and educational performance. Sometimes there are additional committees for pupil well-being.

The model articles of association allow for the trustee board to establish committees. The term trustee committees is used here to distinguish those committees which are made up of trustees and are a direct off-shoot of the trustee board and MAT ACs, which may have no trustees in their membership. In a SAT all committees will have a majority of trustees in membership.

The AFH 2018 requires academy trusts to establish an audit committee and says they should have a finance committee. The audit committee can be part of the finance committee unless the trust has an annual income of over £50m, in which case it must be separate.

Checklist

▷ Check the articles of association for rules on establishing committees and membership.

▷ The trustee board must establish an audit committee – employees should not be members of the audit committee.

▷ The trustee board should establish a finance committee.

▷ In a MAT check the articles for rules about academy committees.

▷ The trustee board must formally approve the establishment of any committees.

▷ The trustee board (subject to articles of association) must to set membership, constitution and terms of reference (i.e. delegated authorities).

▷ The trustee board needs to approve existence and powers of committees at least annually.

▷ Trustees should receive regular reports from committees – this is usually via minutes of committee meetings.

▷ If non-trustees are appointed to trustee committees ensure that the majority of committee members are trustees and that no decisions have been made at meetings where trustees weren't in the majority.

Procedure

▷ Committees need to be approved at a properly convened and quorate trustees' meeting – this must be done annually.

▷ Committee membership, terms of reference and decision-making powers should be part of the SoD.

▷ Minutes of committee meetings must be circulated to trustees – usually as papers for the next trustee meeting.

Notes

▷ Trustees need to consider the best structure to enable them to carry out their duties as trustees and company directors. The AFH is clear that there must be an audit committee to provide robust oversight of financial management.

▷ In SATs it is possible to govern with just the required audit committee. The trustee board will need to meet more than the statutory minimum and possibly every month. It is unlikely to be possible to do this in all but the smallest MATs. Even allowing for academy committees considering some of the dates, the sheer size and complexity of the organisation will make it difficult for the trustee board to properly fulfil its oversight without separate committees.

More information

▷ Academy Governance Checklists:

  ▷ Academy committee – general;
  ▷ Audit Committee;
  ▷ Delegation of authority;
  ▷ Finance Committee;
  ▷ Scheme of delegation (of governance functions).

▷ AFH.

▷ *Academy Governance Handbook*, Chapter 6.

Trustee committees – non-trustee members

Introduction

Most boards operate with some committees in order to manage the workload and detail involved in governing more effectively.

Being a trustee is a responsible and time-consuming role and there are a number of people with the skills but without the time to undertake a full trusteeship.

Maintained schools have long had the power to appoint 'associate members' to committees of the governing body in order to bring in specific skills and expertise. Academy trustee boards also have that power through the articles of association. The articles state that trustees can appoint some non-trustees to committees of the board providing that trustees remain in the majority and no vote can take place unless that is the case.

Using these provisions the trustees can appoint people to committees who can offer skills and expertise but potentially limited time.

Checklist

▶ Check the trust's articles of association, as there are some differences, to see whether it is possible to appoint non-trustees.

▶ Follow any specific rules for appointment – the model articles provide considerable freedom in this.

▶ Trustee board will need to decide whether power to appoint should be delegated to the relevant committee or remain with the full trustee board.

▶ The SoD must detail who can appoint non-trustee committee members.

▶ Consider whether any of the committees lack particular expertise.

▶ Set clear terms of reference and terms of office for non-trustee committee members.

▶ Consider what checks need to be made – e.g. DBS checks.

Procedure

▷ Request the governance professional to put together a proper recruitment package for these roles.

▷ Recruitment should be based on the skills /experience needed for the committee in question.

▷ Recruitment should be carried out following best practice rules.

▷ Carry out relevant check.

▷ Formally appoint.

Notes

▷ This can be a useful option for trustee boards when seeking to provide additional expertise.

▷ Do adopt a proper recruitment process and particularly have clear rules around the term of office. The articles of association leave it to the trustee board to determine the term of office for a non-trustee committee member, these don't have to be the same for all committee members, trustee boards should consider what will be the appropriate term for each appointment. The skills of the board of trustees will change over time, so a gap you had this year might not be the gap you have next year, if you've set the term of office for too long you might restrict your ability to act to fill arising needs. If you set a shorter term of office you can always extend it, but at least won't be in the embarrassing position of having to ask someone to resign or even worse using powers to remove them.

▷ Like any tool it's only effective if used properly, so make the most to the flexibility. Term of office can and should be varied according to the reason you are looking to appoint a non-trustee member. It could be used to appoint someone to help during a project – i.e. during a large building project appoint someone who has expertise in that area to help trustees scrutinise progress (as opposed to operationally project managing). Use the flexibility to appoint to cover the period of the building project.

▷ This flexibility is designed to enable the board to appoint someone to fill gap, something the current trustee board is missing, not just another a voice round the table. Just because you can doesn't mean you should. If the trustee committees are working well then you may not need the option.

▷ Audit committee:

  ▷ One committee where the trustees might wish to consider always having some non-trustees in membership is the audit committee. All academy trusts are required to have audit committees to provide assurance about the trust's financial systems and control. Non-trustees sitting on these committees can be useful in terms of reassurance for trustees, but also for external bodies. In some cases, non-trustees have been appointed to the audit committee in order to provide more 'independence' to that membership. In at least one case the non-trustee was recruited to chair the audit committee.

Filing requirements

None.

More information

▷ Academy Governance Checklists: Trustees – recruitment.

▷ *Academy Governance Handbook*, Chapter 6.

Trustees – appointment

Introduction

The method for appointment of trustees is set out in the articles of association. Different iterations of the articles of association have slightly different categories of trustees.

Checklist

- Check articles of association for any trust-specific eligibility rules for trustee appointments.

- Check articles of association to establish who has the authority to appoint trustees.

- Academy trust trustees must be at least 18 years old.

- Check whether the trustee is disqualified from acting by statute or the articles of association.

- Check whether the declaration of interest raise any concerns/ questions about the ability to act independently – it is good practice to ask for this at recruitment stage.

- Ensure formal checks, i.e. disqualification and DBS checks, have been carried out.

- Ensure any appointment is confirmed by the appropriate body in writing.

Procedure

- The procedure will depend on the articles of association, category of trustee and any trust specific rules.

- Follow the academy trust's director/trustee recruitment procedure.

- Parent trustees – generally by election. Arrange an election in line with the articles and any rules adopted by the academy trust.

▶ Staff trustee – follow the procedures set out in the articles/adopted by the trust (current model articles do not allow for elected staff trustees, but some earlier versions do).

▶ Convene meeting of members/directors depending on which category of director is being appointed. Alternatively, written resolutions can be used.

▶ File completed form AP01 at Companies House.

▶ Update the trust's records via the governance portal on the DfE's GIAS website.

Filing requirements

▶ New trustees are also directors, form AP01 to Companies House.

▶ ESFA need to be informed via the GIAS system.

Notes

▶ The model articles of association do not include a finite length of service, but it is open to trustees to include one as part of their code of conduct – i.e. the expectation is that trustees won't serve more than two to three terms. It is considered good practice to have a finite length of service.

More information

▶ Academy Governance Checklists: Directors – appointment.

▶ Anna Machin's sample trustee appointment checklist (see Appendix).

▶ *Academy Governance Handbook*, Chapter 2.

Trustees – categories

Introduction

The articles of association provide the details of the categories of trustees and the body/person responsible for appointment.

Checklist

The following categories of trustees exist in at least some trusts; not all academy trusts will have all categories. Check the articles to see what categories apply and who has the power to appoint.

▶ Community trustees – in a very few early converter schools the model articles allowed for community trustees. This effectively carried over a category from the maintained sector. Community trustees are appointed by the trustee board. The definition is someone who is committed to the success of the academy trust and lives or works in the community served by the trust.

▶ Co-opted trustees – these are people appointed by the other trustees to enhance the skills, knowledge and experience of the trustee board.

▶ Foundation trustees – some trusts also have another foundation (charitable) body associated with them and this body will usually have the power to appoint trustees –this is often, although not exclusively, a religious body of some kind.

▶ Member-appointed trustees – the articles will specify how many trustees the members may appoint.

▶ Parents – most articles will state that there must be at least two elected parent trustees. In MATs, if there is academy-level governance, the parental requirement can be fulfilled by having parents on ACs rather than the trustee board.

▶ Senior executive leader – earlier versions of the articles gave the senior executive leader an automatic right to be trustee. The current model articles allow the senior executive leader to be a trustee if they agree to serve and the members appoint.

▶ Sponsor trustees – where the trust has a named sponsor body associated with it, the sponsor will usually be allowed to appoint a certain number of trustees. In some cases, this is corporate body and in others a named individual known as the principal sponsor.

▶ Staff – in some earlier versions of the articles there is a position for staff trustees. This does not appear in the current model articles and the AFH makes clear that the DfE does not think it appropriate for staff other than the senior executive leader to be trustees.

Procedure

▶ The procedure for recruitment and appointment will depend on the category of trustee.

More information

▶ Academy Governance Checklists:

  ▷ Directors – appointment;
  ▷ Trustees – appointment;
  ▷ Trustees – recruitment.

▶ *Academy Governance Handbook*, Chapter 1.

Trustees – cessation of office

Introduction

It is considered best practice for there to be turnover on any board, to prevent it getting stale or 'cosy'. The model articles of association do not contain a maximum length of service for academy trustees, so it is up to the trustee board to engineer turnover, it is possible to do this through trustee rules.

In academy trusts trustees and directors have dual roles, consequently the reasons for ceasing office as a trustee are very similar to those as a director.

A trustee may cease to hold office for a variety of reasons:

▶ They may resign – under the model articles a trustee can resign at any point, providing there remain at least three trustees remain in office.

▶ They may come to the end of the term of office – the model articles provide for a four-year term of office. The model articles do not contain a maximum length of service so trustees can be re-elected or reappointed at the end of the four-year term, unless the trustee board has adopted its own maximum.

▶ They may be disqualified from further service as a director/ trustee – the Company Directors Disqualification Act 1986 sets out the circumstances in which a director can be disqualified. (See Disqualification rules, page 124.) If an individual is disqualified as a director they generally be disqualified from acting as a trustee.

▶ They may be removed from office by the person:

▷ who appointed them – a trustee may be removed at any time by the person/persons who appointed them; or
▷ the members – the members of the academy trust have the power to remove any trustee by virtue of the power in the Companies Act for members to remove any director by means of ordinary resolution.

Checklist

▶ Check the articles of association for the rules about removal of trustees.

▶ Written notice must be given to the clerk to the trustees where the trustee resigns or is removed from office.

▶ Companies House must be informed via from TM01 within 14 days.

▶ The ESFA must be informed using the governance portal of GIAS.

▶ The register of directors must be updated.

Procedure

▶ Resignation:

▷ It is best practice to obtain a written letter of resignation.
▷ The clerk to the trustee board must be informed in writing of the resignation.
▷ Ensure the resignation is noted in the minutes of the next relevant meeting.
▷ The ESFA will need to be notified via Get information about schools – within 14 days.
▷ Companies House need to be informed by TM01 within 14 days.
▷ The relevant registers will need to be amended.
▷ Update the trust's website and any other relevant material.

▶ Removal from office:

▷ It is generally better to seek the resignation of a trustee than to use formal removal procedures.

▶ Procedure – removal by an individual or other body entitled to appoint a trustee:

▷ The person or company must write to the clerk informing them of the removal of the trustee.
▷ Minutes of the next trustees meeting should record the removal.
▷ ESFA should be notified via Get information about schools.
▷ Companies House should be informed using form TM01.

▶ Procedure – removal at a board meeting of a director appointed by the board:

▷ The articles do not provide a set process for carrying out this procedure.
▷ Removal requires a formal vote so it should be a stated item of business on the agenda of a meeting.
▷ Convene a meeting of the trustees.
▷ The quorum for a meeting at which it is proposed to remove a trustee is in the model articles is any two-thirds (rounded up to a whole number) of the persons who are at the time trustees present at the meeting and entitled to vote on those respective matters.

▷ The trustee proposed for removal should be given the opportunity to respond to the resolution.

▷ The resolution requires a simple majority.

▷ The clerk to the trustee board must be informed in writing of the removal.

▷ Notify the ESFA within 14 days via governance portal of Get information about schools

▷ Companies House should be informed using TM01.

▶ Procedure – removal by the members:

▷ The members have the power to remove any director of the company by virtue of an ordinary resolution. A director can only be removed at a meeting – i.e. not by written resolution.

▷ Special notice must be given to the company of the proposal to remove a director – notice can be given by the company secretary or a director. Special notices must be issued 28 clear days before the meeting.

▷ A copy of the special notice must be sent to the director whose removal is proposed.

▷ If necessary (i.e. if there is not a scheduled meeting), convene a general meeting of members giving 14 clear days notice. The notice of the general meeting should specify that special notice has been given. The director proposed for removal is entitled to have written representation circulated with the notice.

▷ A simple majority is required to carry the proposal.

▷ If resolution is approved, file form TM01 with Companies House.

▷ The register of directors must be updated.

▷ The ESFA must be notified within 14 days via the GIAS website.

▶ Other cessations of office:

▷ Most of the steps set out under resignation procedure will apply.

Filing requirements

▶ Form TM01 to Companies House within 14 days.

▶ ESFA via the GIAS website – within 14 days.

More information

▶ Academy Governance Checklists: Disqualification rules (for members, trustees, directors and those on academy committees).

▶ *Academy Governance Handbook*, Chapter 4.

Trustees – duties

Introduction

The trustees of an academy trust hold a legal position as charity trustees. Charity trustees have legally defined responsibilities, not to mention that those running charities are expected to be held to the highest standards of expected behaviour.

In academy trusts, trustees have overlapping responsibilities as charity trustee and company directors.

Checklist

The Charity Commission's guidance document the *Essential trustee* states that trustees have independent control over, and legal responsibility for, a charity's management and administration. The document goes on to set out the core responsibilities for all charity trustees in more detail. These are to:

▶ ensure your charity is carrying out its purposes for the public benefit:

  ▷ ensure you understand the charity's purposes as set out in its governing document;

  ▷ plan what your charity will do, and what you want it to achieve;

  ▷ be able to explain how all the charity's activities are intended to further or support its purposes;

▶ understand how the charity benefits the public by carrying out its purposes:

  ▷ comply with your charity's governing document and the law;

  ▷ make sure your charity complies with its governing document;

  ▷ comply with charity law requirements and other laws that apply to your charity;

▶ act in your charity's best interests:

  ▷ do what you and your co-trustees (and no one else) decide will best enable the charity to carry out its purposes;

  ▷ with your co-trustees make balanced and adequate informed decisions, thinking about the long term as well as the short term;

▷ avoid putting yourself in a position where your duty to your charity conflicts with your personal interests or loyalty to another body;

▷ do not receive any benefit from your charity unless it is properly authorised and is clearly in the charity's interests; this also includes anyone who is financially connected to you, such as a partner, dependent child or business partner;

▶ manage your charity's resources responsibly:

▷ make sure your charity's assets are only used to support or carry out its purpose;

▷ avoid exposing the charity's assets, beneficiaries or reputation to undue risk;

▷ do not overcommit the charity;

▷ take special care when investing or borrowing;

▷ comply with any restrictions on spending funds or selling land;

▶ act with reasonable care and skill:

▷ must use reasonable care and skill, making use of your skills and experience and taking appropriate advice when necessary;

▷ should give enough time, thought and energy to your role, for example by preparing for, attending and actively participating in all trustees' meetings;

▶ ensure your charity is accountable:

▷ be able to demonstrate that your charity is complying with the law, and is well run and effective;

▷ ensure appropriate accountability to your members, if your charity has a membership separate from the trustees; and

▷ ensure accountability within the charity, particularly where you delegate responsibility for particular tasks or decisions to staff or volunteers.

Procedures

▶ The procedures to be followed will be subject to the articles of association, the CA2006 and any requirements of the DfE and ESFA.

Notes

▶ All trustees should be familiar with their duties as charitable trustee and company directors, this should form part of the induction process.

More information

▶ Academy Governance Checklists: Directors – duties.

▶ *Academy Governance Handbook*, Chapter 4.

Trustees – induction

Introduction

Induction provides an opportunity to welcome the new trustee and ensure they have the knowledge and support to fulfil their role effectively. All trustees should undergo induction.

A clear expectation should be placed on all trustees that they will undergo induction.

Checklist

▶ The governance professional should develop an induction programme.

▶ Recruitment material should make clear that new trustees will be expected to undertake induction.

▶ Arrange for the chair and senior executive leader to be available on induction days.

▶ Induction should cover:

▷ roles and responsibilities;
▷ structure of the trust, governance and operational structure; and
▷ strategic priorities, financial position of the trust and key challenges.

Procedure

▶ Trustees to agree an induction procedure – the governance professional should be integral to developing this.

▶ Trustees to agree who will lead – governance professional/chair.

▶ Arrange dates with the new trustee.

Notes

▶ The precise format of the induction should vary with the knowledge skills and experience of the new trustee.

▷ A trustee who has been a charitable trustee elsewhere will need less information/development in relation to the formal duties and responsibilities but may know little of the vagaries of the educational setting. Alternatively, a new trustee who has managed or governed in the maintained sector may know quite a lot about how schools work, but not be so familiar with the responsibilities of directors/trustees.

▷ All trustees will need an induction which covers the specific workings of their trust. This should include who their fellow trustees are, the number and membership of any committees, both trust and AC, the organisational structure and financial position.

Trustees – recruitment

Introduction

All academy trusts will need to fill trustee vacancies at some point. it is vital that there are procedures in place to ensure that the right people can be recruited. The right people being those who have the commitment, experience, skills and time to provide the leadership and scrutiny the role requires. The experience and skills will vary depending on the make-up of the rest of the board – commitment and time will always be essential.

Checklist

▶ Maintain a record of trustees' terms of office so recruitment for a replacement can start early.

▶ Check any eligibility criteria specific to the vacancy – e.g. parents/staff.

▶ Ensure board skills audit is up to date to enable recruitment to fill any gaps – the AFH 2018 requires trusts to identify any skills gap and fill them through recruitment or training.

▶ Recruitment literature should include details of: eligibility and disqualification criteria, declaration of interest forms, trustee code of conduct, role description and expected time commitment.

▶ Advertise the vacancy as widely as possible: trust's website, social media, trustee recruitment sites and possibly the press.

▶ Prospective trustees should be asked to sign a declaration of eligibility.

▶ Interviews – arrange time and place and ensure trustee interview panel is available.

▶ Recruitment services:

▷ Academy ambassadors – government funded – set up specifically to recruit trustees for MATs: www.academyambassadors.org
▷ Inspiring Governance – government-funded service – governors/trustees for single schools and academy committees: www.inspiringgovernance.org/recruiting-governors

> Governors for schools – charitable organisation – recruits governors/trustees for all types of state-funded schools and academies: www.governorsforschools.org.uk
> Others – there are a range of charity trustee recruitment services not specific to any sector.

Procedure

▶ The procedure will depend on the vacancy being recruited to, requirements of the articles of association and any recruitment procedure adopted by the board.

▶ Prospective trustees should be checked against eligibility criteria.

▶ Interviewing – if the appointment is subject to interview a venue will need to be arranged and panel members briefed.

▶ Confirmation – prospective trustees will need to be formally appointed by the relevant body – members/trustees.

Filing requirements

None at this stage – once appointment there will be filing requirements at Companies House and the GIAS website.

Notes

▶ Evidence from other sectors show that diverse boards improve effectiveness. It is good practice for the trustee board to approach trustee recruitment as they would for staff posts, by adopting a formal process, applications and interviews. The NGA, in conjunction with Inspiring Governance, has produced a recruitment guide for governing boards.

▶ There is no national statistical collection about the characteristics of those governing in the state-funded sector; the best source of information comes from the NGA/TES annual survey and that shows lack of ethnic diversity and very few governing below the age of 35.

▶ There are three dedicated governor/trustee recruitment services for schools.

▶ Once appointed, trustees must fill in a declaration of interests, but it is good practice to request this as part of the recruitment process. Having the information at the start of the process highlights any potential issues. If candidates are new to trusteeship they may not have considered the potential for conflict of interest and they may withdraw of their own volition. For trustee boards it enables them to 'avoid' a conflict by not proceeding to appointment rather than try to manage it after the fact.

▶ Some trustees are appointed by other bodies, i.e. sponsor or foundation body, and the trustee board has no automatic say in that process.

▶ Members have the right in the articles to appoint a certain number of trustees. Trustees should seek to agree a process with members for recommending candidates for appointment by members. Best practice would be following a similar recruitment to that used by the trustees for their own co-options, i.e. by advertisement, application and interview. The trustees could then recommend candidates to members. A member could potentially sit on the interview panel.

More information

▶ Academy Governance Checklists:

▷ Competency Framework for Governance (DfE);
▷ Directors – appointment;
▷ Trustees – appointment;
▷ Trustees – recruitment.

▶ *Academy Governance Handbook*, Chapter 4.

UK Corporate Governance Code

Introduction

The UK Corporate Governance Code was revised and following consultation and a new version in 2018.

The code sets out standards of good governance over five headings. Listed companies must report against the code, but private companies such as academy trusts are encouraged to comply.

Checklist

▶ The UK Corporate Governance Code is organised around five key areas boards should focus on; under each area is a set of principles and then more detailed provisions for boards to consider. The headline areas and examples of principles are set out below.

▶ Board leadership and company purpose:

▷ A successful company is led by an effective and entrepreneurial board, whose role is to promote the long-term sustainable success of the company, generating value for shareholders and contributing to wider society.

▶ Division of responsibilities:

▷ The chair leads the board and is responsible for its overall effectiveness in directing the company.

▶ Audit, risk and internal control:

▷ The board should establish formal and transparent policies and procedures to ensure the independence and effectiveness of internal and external audit functions and satisfy itself on the integrity of financial and narrative statements.

▶ Remuneration:

▷ Remuneration policies and practices should be designed to support strategy and promote long-term sustainable success. Executive remuneration should be aligned to company purpose and values and be clearly linked to the successful delivery of the company's long-term strategy.

Procedure

▷ The board should consider the provisions of the code as part of any review of their practice and effectiveness.

Filing requirements

None.

More information

▷ Academy Governance Checklists:

   ▷ Charity Governance Code;
   ▷ Good Governance Standard for Public Services.

▷ *Academy Governance Handbook*, Chapter 1.

University Technical Colleges

Introduction

UTCs are a type of free school and consequently academies. They provide more technical based education for pupils aged 14–19.

All UTCs are run under licence from the Baker Dearing Trust and articles of association for trusts containing UTCs contain specific requirements about the composition of the board of trustee or relevant AC.

Checklist

▶ UTCs may be SATs or MATs.

▶ Check that approval has been granted from the Baker Dearing Trust for prospective academy to operate as a UTC.

▶ Ensure provisions of articles in relation to 'employer and 'university' sponsors are met.

  ▷ SATs – model articles provide for nominees of 'employer sponsor' and 'university sponsor' always constitute a majority of trustees.
  ▷ MATs – require that the AC established for the UTC has a majority of 'employer sponsor' and 'university sponsor' nominees.

▶ Model articles of association require that the Baker Dearing Trust be consulted if the trustees establish any byelaws which impact directly upon the UTC.

Procedure

▶ The procedure will vary according to whether a UTC is being established as a SAT or as part of a MAT.

▶ Ongoing trustee/academy committee recruitment procedures need to make provision for the employer and university sponsor clauses.

Filing requirements

▶ This will depend on what process is being undertaken.

Notes

▶ UTCs are championed by Lord Baker and the trust he established; the Baker Dearing Trust has a formal role in licensing them.

▶ A number of UTCs have struggled and subsequently closed, mainly as a result of failing to attract enough students, which affected their long-term viability.

Value Added Tax

Introduction

VAT is a tax charged on a variety of goods and services and applies to most business transactions. There are three rates of VAT depending on the services provided.

Companies, including academy trusts can register for VAT, which enables them to reclaim VAT. Companies not registered for VAT can reclaim VAT paid on goods and services using a specific form, but are not allowed to charge VAT.

There is a threshold above which companies must register for VAT which is based on taxable turnover.

State-funded education holds a special position in relation to VAT.

Checklist

▷ Ensure the academy trust is meeting the regulations in relation to payment, charging and reclamation of VAT.

▷ Ensure specialist professional advice is available to operational staff and trustees as necessary.

Procedure

▷ Trustees may need to authorise procurement of specialist VAT advice.

▷ Ensure robust financial procedures are in place.

Notes

▷ VAT is a notoriously complicated area and as academy trusts are private companies providing state-funded education they occupy a particularly specialist niche. It is essential specialist professional advice is sought in relation to VAT.

More information

▷ HMRC VAT for academies: www.gov.uk/hmrc-internal-manuals/vat-education-manual/vatedu70000

Website publication requirements

Introduction

All academy trusts are required to have a website and in the case of MATs websites for individual academies.

The academy trust is required by various legislation and guidance, principally funding agreements, The Education (Independent School Standards) Regulations 2014 and the AFH to publish certain information on its websites.

Academy trusts are also subject to the FOI Act.

Checklist

▶ Check the funding agreement(s) – different versions contain different requirements – and publish accordingly.

▶ Ensure that the academy trust has published all required information. Information to be published will generally fall under the following headings; for some trusts this will be a requirement of their funding agreement and for others optional but considered good practice. In MATs some information should be published on individual academy websites.

▷ School or college contact details.
▷ Admission arrangements.
▷ Ofsted reports.
▷ Exam and assessment results.
▷ Performance tables.
▷ Curriculum.
▷ Behaviour policy.
▷ Pupil premium.
▷ Year 7 literacy and numeracy catch-up premium.
▷ PE and sport premium for primary schools.
▷ Special educational needs and disabilities (SEND).
▷ Careers programme information.
▷ Equality objectives.
▷ Complaints policy.
▷ Annual reports and accounts.

▷ Trustees' information and duties.
▷ Charging and remissions policies.
▷ Values and ethos.

Procedure

▶ Maintain a list of what needs to be published and when it needs to be reviewed/updated.

Filing requirements

None.

Notes

▶ Where the funding agreement does not contain a requirement to publish information, but, if the trust had opened at a later date, it would, it is considered good practice to publish.

More information

▶ DfE – information academies should publish: www.gov.uk/guidance/what-academies-free-schools-and-colleges-should-publish-online

▶ *Academy Governance Handbook*, Chapter 9.

Working together to safeguard children and young people

Introduction

Working together to safeguard children and young people is the government's overarching safeguarding guidance for all organisations with responsibility for safeguarding children and young people. It acts in conjunction with the sector-specific KCSIE.

This guidance focuses on the core legal requirements, making it clear what individuals, organisations and agencies must and should do to keep children safe.

Checklist

▷ Academy trusts are required by the Education (Independent School Standards) 2014 to have regard to any guidance the Secretary of State issues in relation to safeguarding and child protection. *Working together* is statutory guidance.

▷ The document applies in its entirety to all schools, including academies.

▷ Academy trusts must comply with its requirements.

▷ Trustees should also be familiar with the relevant sections of KCSIE.

Notes

▷ Safeguarding is a critical responsibility of the trustee board. *Working together* sets out that all those involved in safeguarding should co-operate to ensure vulnerable children are identified and supported.

More information

▷ *Working together to safeguard children*: www.gov.uk/government/publications/working-together-to-safeguard-children—2

Appendix – Sample multi-academy trust trustee appointment and induction checklist

Trustee appointment checklist

No.	Action	Done?
1	Complete Disclosure & Barring Service (DBS) check. *If Board Chair – ensure copy of Chair's DBS is signed by Secretary of State.*	
2	Complete trust Declaration of Interest, Declaration of Eligibility and Code of Conduct form. *If Board Chair appointment - also complete ID Verification Check.*	
3	Conduct eligibility check through public Insolvency and Disqualified Directors registers in relation to automatic disqualification rules.	
4	Trustee to confirm read Keeping Children Safe in Education Part One and complete required Safeguarding training.	
5	Secure Secretary of State approval (if required by trust's Master Funding Agreement).	
6	Notify DfE/ESFA of trustee appointment within 14 days by updating 'Get Information About Schools' (GIAS).	
7	Notify Companies House of trustee appointment within 14 days through AP01 webfiling form.	
8	Add biography to trust website Trustees page.	
9	Add trustee's details to Register of Directors.	
10	Add trustee's Declaration of Interest to Register of Interests and summary of interests to document published on trust website.	
11	Add trustee email address to board and other relevant mailing lists.	
12	Ensure Trustee is included in trust Directors' insurance arrangements.	
13	Create, share, arrange Chair signature and file signed appointment letter.	
14	Notify management team and other relevant staff of appointment completion.	

Trustee induction checklist

No.	Action	Done?
1	Meet key personnel – schedule meeting with Board Chair, CEO, CFO, education and operations directors, Company Secretary and other relevant team members. *These are best scheduled around pre-existing commitments e.g. immediately before/ after a Board meeting.*	
2	Understand general MAT trustee legal duties – signpost to (1) DfE Governance Handbook, (2) DfE Competency Framework for Governance, (3) DfE Academies Financial Handbook, (4) Charity Commission 'The Essential Trustee'.	
3	Understand MAT sector – signpost to useful documents such as the DfE Introduction to Schools Finance, NGA Glossary of Education Terms and Academy Ambassadors Introduction to Academy Data.	
4	Understand trustee legal duties as they apply to the trust – send (1) signed Trustee Appointment Letter, (2) Articles of Association, (3) Master Funding Agreement, (4) Scheme of Delegation, (5) Financial Delegated Authorities, (6) Terms of Reference for Board, Committees and local governance.	
5	Understand legal support – (7) Code of Conduct, Whistleblowing and Conflicts of Interest policies (and any others requested), (8) trust governance and legal contact details, (9) directors' insurance details.	
6	Understand Ark Schools vision and strategy – attach (10) current-year operating plan, (11) prior-year academic results, (12) prior-year annual report and accounts, (13) current high-level risk register, (14) senior leadership structure chart, (15) media coverage booklet.	
7	Understand background to Board delivery – attach (16) annual calendar of key events/ deadlines e.g. meetings, annual return, key stage results, (17) current-year agenda planner, (18) 6 × most recent Board meeting minutes, (19) results of most recent Board self-evaluation, signpost to (20) Board biographies and register of interests on website, (21) biographies of Committee members, (22) summary of Committee self-evaluation(s).	
8	Set up logistical aspects – send invites to (a) Board meetings, (b) key events e.g. Headteacher's meetings, Chair's forums, (c) planned trustee training.	

Directory of web resources

Government departments, inspectorates, non-departmental public bodies and regulators

Education bodies

DfE: www.gov.uk/government/organisations/department-for-education

ESFA: www.gov.uk/government/organisations/education-and-skills-funding-agency

Ofqual: www.gov.uk/government/organisations/ofqual

Ofsted: www.gov.uk/government/organisations/ofsted

STA: www.gov.uk/government/organisations/standards-and-testing-agency

Non-education bodies

Charity Commission: www.gov.uk/government/organisations/charity-commission

Companies House: www.gov.uk/government/organisations/companies-house

Disclosure and Barring Service: www.gov.uk/government/organisations/disclosure-and-barring-service

Health and Safety Executive: www.hse.gov.uk

HMRC: www.gov.uk/government/organisations/hm-revenue-customs

Information Commissioner's Office: www.ico.org.uk

National Audit Office: www.nao.org.uk

Parliamentary bodies

Education Committee: www.parliament.uk/business/committees/committees-a-z/commons-select/education-committee

Public Accounts Committee: www.parliament.uk/business/committees/committees-a-z/commons-select/public-accounts-committee

Representative organisations

Academy/school governance

National Governance Association: www.nga.org.uk

Confederation of School Trusts: www.cstuk.org.uk

Governance professionals – cross sector

ICSA: The Governance Institute: www.icsa.org.uk

Professional associations/trade union (education)

ASCL: www.ascl.org.uk

NAHT: www.naht.org.uk

Institute of School Business Leaders: www.isbl.org.uk

National Education Union: www.neu.org.uk

NASUWT: www.nasuwt.org.uk

Voice: www.voicetheunion.org.uk

Academy/school governor recruitment organisations

Academy Ambassadors: www.academyambassadors.org

Governors for schools: www.governorsforschools.org.uk

Inspiring Governance: www.inspiringgovernance.org

Other organisations

Catholic Education Service: www.catholiceducation.org.uk

Church of England Education Office (National Society): www.churchofengland.org/more/education-and-schools

New Schools Network: www.newschoolsnetwork.org

Other useful sites

Legislation: www.legislation.gov.uk

Specific useful resources

Board evaluation

All Party Parliamentary Group:

–   Twenty key questions for the governing board to ask itself: www.nga.org.uk/Knowledge-Centre/Good-governance/Effective-governance/Twenty-Questions.aspx

- Twenty-one key questions a MAT board should ask itself: www.nga.org.uk/Knowledge-Centre/Governance-structure-roles-and-responsibilities/Multi-academy-trusts/Twenty-one-Questions-for-Multi-academy-Trust-Board.aspx

ICSA Academy School Governance Maturity Matrix: www.icsa.org.uk/knowledge/resources/academy-school-maturity-matrix

ICSA Multi-academy trust governance – board effectiveness: www.icsa.org.uk/knowledge/resources/mat-board-effectiveness

Charity Commission

The Essential Trustee: www.gov.uk/government/publications/the-essential-trustee-what-you-need-to-know-cc3

DfE

Clerking competency framework; Competency framework for governance; and Governance Handbook: www.gov.uk/government/publications/governance-handbook

Schools causing concern guidance: www.gov.uk/government/publications/schools-causing-concern--2

ESFA academy information and resources

Academies Financial Handbook: www.gov.uk/government/publications/academies-financial-handbook

Academies: funding, payments and compliance: www.gov.uk/government/collections/academies-funding-payments-and-compliance

Governance codes

Charity Governance Code: www.charitygovernancecode.org/en/front-page

Nolan Principles and Framework for Ethical Leadership in Education:

- The Nolan Principles (the 7 principles of public life): www.gov.uk/government/publications/the-7-principles-of-public-life

- Navigating the Educational Moral Maze (Ethical Leadership Commission report): www.ascl.org.uk/utilities/document-summary.html?id=6FEEA19D-EC2F-46E5-A42A61D83FA7C4C8

UK Corporate Governance Code: www.frc.org.uk/directors/corporate-governance-and-stewardship/uk-corporate-governance-code

Index

Lightning Source UK Ltd.
Milton Keynes UK
UKHW020455160920
369908UK00003B/184